# *Wrapped* IN CROCHET

## Scarves, Wraps & Shawls

Kristin Omdahl

INTERWEAVE
interweavebooks.com

**EDITOR:** Katrina Loving

**TECH EDITORS:** Julie Holetz and Karen Manthey

**PHOTOGRAPHY:** Brooks Freehill

**ART DIRECTION+COVER DESIGN:** Connie Poole

**INTERIOR DESIGN:** Stacy Ebright

**PRODUCTION DESIGN:** Katherine Jackson

**HAIR & MAKEUP:** Catherine Corona

Text © 2008 Kristin Omdahl

Photography © 2008 Interweave Press LLC

Photographs on pages 34 and 35 used with permission from Jennifer Hansen at Stitch Diva Studios, stitchdiva.com

Interweave Press LLC
201 East Fourth Street
Loveland, CO 80537-5655 USA
interweavebooks.com

Printed in China by Asia Pacific Offset

Library of Congress Cataloging-in-Publication Data

Omdahl, Kristin.

  Wrapped in crochet : scarves, wraps, and shawls / Kristin Omdahl, author.

    p. cm.

  Includes index.

  ISBN 978-1-59668-076-0 (pbk.)

  1. Crocheting--Patterns. 2. Scarves. 3. Shawls. I. Title.

  TT825.O44 2008

  746.43'4041--dc22

2008014302

10  9  8  7  6  5  4  3  2  1

# *acknowledgments*

**Special thanks to:**

The Crochet Girls (Jennifer Carabio, Christine Clever-Scheuer, Melissa Kelly, Debra Lane, Gail Moehlman, Christine Penzak, Tina Robbins, Dhurat Rosinski, Patti Smith, and Jen Yohe) for their meticulously stitched sample garments, incredible attention to detail, a fun crochet party, and lots of triangle motifs!

John, for being an angel when we needed one.

*To Marlon, my inspiration*

# table of *contents*

# introduction

When I taught myself how to crochet, it was out of necessity: I was pregnant, living overseas with practically no support for the craft, and compelled to make booties and blankets for my child's impending arrival. I worked from one little pamphlet my mom shipped to me from the States and made several layette sets before realizing that my son was about to be born in a tropical climate in the summertime. I'm afraid that he only wore the outfits once, on a day when I cranked the air-conditioning so he could don my outfits for a little photo shoot. It was only a few minutes—I assure you he did not suffer a bit!

In spite of the fact that my first foray into crochet didn't go exactly as planned, the crochet bug had bitten me, and hard. I was completely obsessed with crochet but had no more booties, layettes, or blankets left to make. What was a mother to do? Always a fan of wraps and shawls, I decided to focus on adult accessories instead. I designed and crocheted a rectangular wrap for my mom. I first made a swatch, then sat down with a calculator, pen, and paper, and figured out how many stitches and rows I needed to create the wrap I wanted to make for her. Always a math addict at heart, I was thrilled to be calculating shapes again. So I wondered if I could calculate other shapes as well, like a triangle. I combined crochet with the Pythagorean theorem. Fireworks exploded in the sky, light bulbs went off over my head, and my passion for crochet design began. I have been consumed, passionate, and thrilled with designing in crochet ever since.

When I was six thousand miles away from my family, I made it a point to crochet every single stitch of a wrap with love and thoughts of the person I missed. It helped me to bridge the gap between myself and the people that I loved. Fast-forward to today, and as a designer of knit and crochet patterns and garments, I am still in love with designing. I am consumed with stitching, geometry, and fiber choices. I am giddy with anticipation with every new project. Seriously.

I am thrilled to write this book full of scarves, wraps, and shawls. It's where I began, and where I fell in love with the craft. Whether you crochet for yourself or the people in your life, make it a point to crochet every stitch with love. Your recipients will feel your hug every time they are wrapped in crochet.

—Kristin

**THERE ARE SO MANY WONDERFUL REASONS**

to crochet scarves: they are often quick and easy projects, they make wonderful gifts for any age, and everyone loves them! In the following chapter, you will find scarves for all different tastes, from simple and classic to funky and unique. Each pattern utilizes a different—and sometimes unusual—technique, including corkscrews, weaving, hairpin lace, and more. Explore the following pages for something you may want to try for the first time. A scarf project is the perfect size to learn something new, and you'll add a new accessory to your wardrobe as well!

# scarves

## materials

**YARN:** Worsted weight (#4 Medium), 800 yd (731.5 m).

*Shown:* Trendsetter Yarns, Tonalita (52% wool/48% acrylic; 100 yd [91 m]/1.75 oz [50 g]): # 2345 flower blossom, 8 balls.

## notions

Tapestry needle

## hook

H/8 (5mm) or size needed to obtain gauge.

## gauge

16 sts and 16 rows = 4" (10 cm) in sc.

## finished size

9½" wide x 70" long (24 cm x 178 cm).

*I love lots of color,* but I don't love weaving in all the loose ends! Playing around with different directions and shapes with self-striping yarn, I inadvertently crocheted a log-cabin motif. Using two different sizes of motifs (one half the size of the other), I found that they fit together perfectly (and easily) when sewn together. Visually, the combination of colors, stripes, and different directions that come together in this cozy scarf are mesmerizing.

*labyrinth*

## NOTES

- For instructions on **Foundation Single Crochet (fsc)**, see p. 115.

- Using a self-striping yarn creates the many subtle color changes seen in this scarf.

*Diagram A*

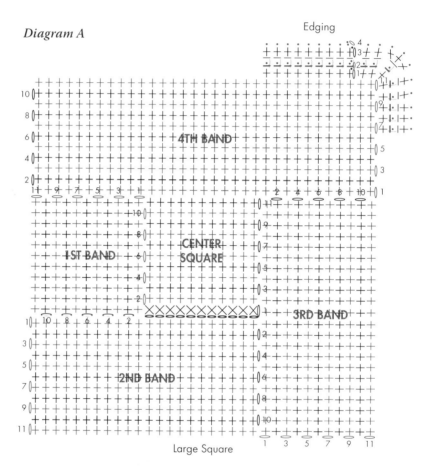

### Stitch Key

⬭ = chain (ch)

• = slip stitch (sl st)

✛ = single crochet (sc)

✗⬭ = foundation single crochet (fsc)

— = worked in back loop only

━ = worked in front loop only

## LARGE SQUARE *(make 6)*
See Diagram A at left for assistance.

### *Center Square*
**ROW 1:** Fsc 11, turn.

**ROW 2:** Ch 1, sc in each st across, turn.

**ROWS 3–11:** Rep Row 2.

### *1st Band*
**ROW 1:** Rotate square 90 degrees clockwise to work in end of rows, ch 1, sc in each end of row of Center Square, turn—11 sts.

**ROWS 2–11:** Ch 1, sc in each st across, turn.

### *2nd Band*
**ROW 1:** Rotate square 90 degrees clockwise, ch 1, sc in each end of row across 1st Band and in each free loop of fsc, turn—22 sts.

**ROWS 2–11:** Ch 1, sc in each st across, turn.

### *3rd Band*
**ROW 1:** Rotate square 90 degrees clockwise, ch 1, sc in each end of row across 2nd Band and Center Square, turn—22 sts.

**ROWS 2–11:** Ch 1, sc in each st across, turn.

### *4th Band*
**ROW 1:** Rotate square 90 degrees clockwise, ch 1, sc in each end of row and in each st across 3rd Band, Center Square and 1st Band, turn—33 sts.

**ROWS 2–11:** Ch 1, sc in each st across, turn.

Fasten off.

### SMALL SQUARE *(make 10)*
See Diagram B on p. 15
for assistance.

#### Center Square
ROW 1: Fsc 5, turn.

ROWS 2–5: Ch 1, sc in each st across, turn.

#### 1st Band
ROW 1: Rotate square 90 degrees clockwise to work in end of rows, ch 1, sc in each end of row across Center Square, turn — 5 sts.

ROWS 2–5: Ch 1, sc in each st across, turn.

#### 2nd Band
ROW 1: Rotate square 90 degrees clockwise to work in end of rows, ch 1, sc in each end of row across 1st Band and in each free loop of beg fsc, turn—10 sts.

ROWS 2–5: Ch 1, sc in each st across, turn.

#### 3rd Band
ROW 1: Rotate square 90 degrees clockwise, ch 1, sc in each end of row across 2nd Band and Center Square, turn—10 sts.

ROWS 2–5: Ch 1, sc in each st across, turn.

#### 4th Band
ROW 1: Rotate square 90 degrees clockwise, ch 1, sc in each end of row and in each st across 3rd Band, Center Square, and 1st Band, turn—15 sts.

ROWS 2–5: Ch 1, sc in each st across, turn.

Fasten off.

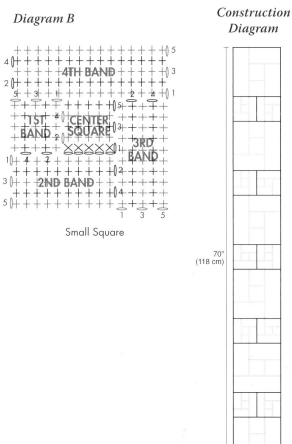

*Diagram B*

4TH BAND

1ST BAND   CENTER SQUARE   3RD BAND

2ND BAND

Small Square

*Construction Diagram*

70"
(118 cm)

9½"
(24 cm)

## FINISHING

With RS facing, sew the motifs together following the Construction Diagram above right.

### Edging

RND 1: Join yarn with sl st to any st around the perimeter of the scarf, ch 1, sc in same st, sc in each st and each end of row around, placing 3 sc in each corner, sl st in flo of first sc to join.

RND 2: *Ch 1, sl st-flo in first st and in each st around, sl st in blo of first st from Rnd 1.

RND 3: Working in free back loops of Rnd 1, ch 1, sc in each st around, working 3 sc into each corner st, sl st into first sc to join.

RND 4: *Ch 1, sl st in first st and in each st around, sl st in first sl st to join. Fasten off.

Handwash, block to finished measurements, and let dry.

**VARIATION:** This pattern can easily be modified to make a wrap. If you double the amount of blocks, the width will double to 19" (48 cm). Just double the amount of yarn required and you've got a Labyrinth Wrap!

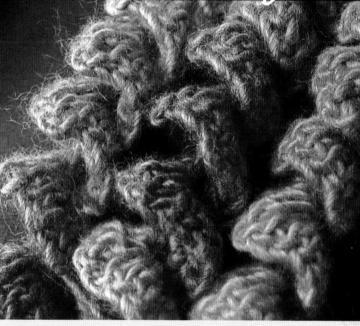

# blaze
## CORKSCREW SCARF

## materials

**YARN:** Worsted weight (#4 Medium), 600 yd (548.6 m).

*Shown:* Patons, SWS (70% wool, 30% soy; 110 yd [100 m]/2.8 oz [80 g]): #70532 natural crimson, 6 balls.

## notions

Tapestry needle

## hook

I/9 (5.5mm) or size needed to obtain gauge.

## gauge

16 sts and 4 rows = 4" (10 cm) in dc.

## finished size

3" wide x 82" long (7.5 cm x 208.3 cm).

*I have never been happy* with a super-skinny scarf. Because I love the texture of corkscrews, I decided to use that as a starting point to create a chunkier scarf. I crocheted a few long corkscrews and strung them together with strategically placed chains and slip stitches, creating the traditional silhouette of a scarf, with a twist. Named for the smoldering effects of the fiery reds and oranges of the self-striping yarn, this corkscrew scarf is funky but also functional.

*Diagram A*

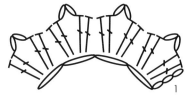

1

*Corkscrew When Coiled*

**Stitch Key**

⬭ = chain (ch)

T = double crochet (dc)

---

**NOTE**

The scarf looks more interesting if the strips are not all the same length. Keep the lengths of the strips within an inch or two of each other to give the scarf subtle variation at the edges.

---

## CORKSCREWS *(make 3)*

See Diagram A above for sample of corkscrew patt.

Ch 390.

**ROW 1:** (2 dc, ch 2, 2 dc) in 4th ch from hook and in each ch across. As you go, the yarn may start to corkscrew upon itself, or you may want to encourage it by twisting as you go. Fasten off.

## FINISHING

Pay attention to the direction of the strips when you lay them out in front of you. The side with the last st, where you fastened off, should be on the right.

### First Joining Row

Lay each strip on a table horizontally in front of you with the first one closest to you and the third one farthest from you. Counting from the left, join yarn with sl st to exposed stitch between the 10th and 11th corkscrew wrap on the first strip, *ch 5, join yarn with sl st to the exposed st between the 10th and 11th corkscrew wrap on the second strip; rep from * with last strip. Fasten off.

### Next Joining Row

When working the next joining row, you are counting wraps from the last sl st joining row, not from the beg of the strip. (See Corkscrew When Coiled diagram at left for assistance.)

**Count 10 corkscrew wraps to the left of the last joining row, join yarn with sl st to the exposed stitch between the 10th and 11th corkscrew wrap, *ch 5, join to next strip with sl st to the exposed st between the 10th and 11th corkscrew wrap; rep from * with last strip. Fasten off.

Rep from ** seven more times or until you have about 10 additional corkscrew (wraps before the end of each strip. If not, it is easy to unfasten the tail and either ravel back a few wraps to shorten the strip or work a few more corkscrew wraps to lengthen the strips.

### FINISHING

Handwash, block to finished measurements, and let dry.

**VARIATIONS:** This scarf can be easily modified for different sizes. Each 82" x 1" (2 m x 2.5 cm) strip uses 195 yd (178.3 m) of the specified yarn.

If you wanted to make this scarf into a wrap that measures about 60" (152.5 cm) long x 16" (40.5 cm) wide, you would need to make 16 corkscrew strips, and the starting chain would be 286 chains. The yardage would decrease to 145 yd (132.5 m) per strip, or 145 yd (132.5 m) x 16 = 2,320 total yardage (2,121 m).

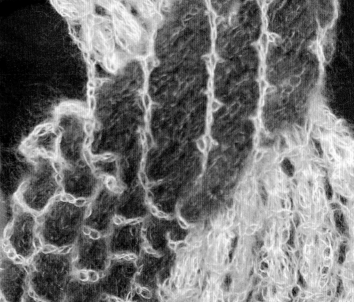

# heidi

## WOVEN & BRAIDED SCARF

## materials

**YARN:** DK weight (#3 Light), 230 yd (210 m) ea of A, B, and C—690 yd (630.9 m) total.

*Shown:* Rowan, Kid Silk Haze (70% super kid mohair, 30% silk; 230 yd [210 m]/1 oz [25 g]): #630 fondant (A); #580 grace (B); #600 dewberry (C), 1 ball each.

## notions

Tapestry needle

## hook

G/6 (4mm) or size needed to obtain gauge.

## gauge

6 mesh boxes and 9 rows = 4" (10 cm).

## finished size

8" wide x 43" long (20.5 cm x 109 cm).

*Several years ago,* I designed a large plaid floor pillow with a mesh background and knitted I-cord "ribbons" woven through it, as a special gift. The Heidi scarf is a continuation of that technique of "woven" crochet. Here, I shaped the mesh "canvas" to duplicate the shape created when the crocheted ribbons are not only woven but also crossed over each other like a knitted cable. By alternating the crossing of colors, the finished scarf appears cabled.

## Stitch Key

◯ = chain (ch)

• = slip st (sl st)

$\dagger$ = double crochet (dc)

$\ddagger$ = treble crochet (tr)

## Diagram A

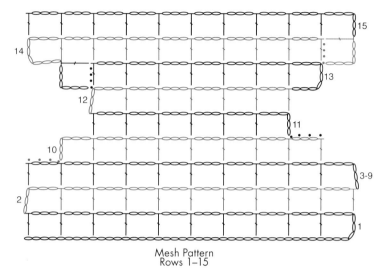

Mesh Pattern
Rows 1–15

## Diagram B

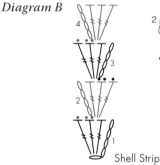

Shell Strip

## Construction Diagram

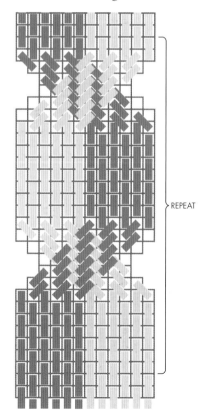

REPEAT

## NOTE

When weaving shell strips through mesh, whichever color is woven second will only be woven through the bars of mesh facing you. Do not dig below the strips to find more mesh pieces for weaving. Ideally, you only want to see the top color (from either side) of the crossings.

## MESH

See Diagram A above for assistance.

With A, ch 54.

ROW 1: Skip 9 ch (counts as ch 3, dc, ch 3), dc in next ch from hook, *ch 3, skip 3 ch, dc in next ch; rep from * to end, turn—12 mesh boxes.

ROW 2: Ch 6 (counts as dc, ch 3), dc in next dc, *ch 3, dc in next dc; rep from * across, working last dc in 4th ch of beg ch-7, turn—12 mesh boxes.

ROW 3–9: Rep Row 2.

ROW 10: Sl st in each of next 3 ch and next dc, ch 6 (counts as dc, ch 3), dc in next dc, *ch 3, dc in next dc; rep from * 8 more times, leaving the last ch-3 and dc unworked, turn—10 mesh boxes.

ROW 11: Sl st in each of the next 3 ch and next dc, ch 7 (counts as dc, ch 3), dc in next dc, *ch 3, dc in next dc; rep from * 6 more times, leaving the last ch-3 and dc unworked, turn—8 mesh boxes.

ROW 12: Rep Row 2—8 mesh boxes.

ROW 13: Ch 9 (count as ch 3, dc, ch 3), dc in first dc, *ch 3, dc in next dc; rep from * across, sl st down to base of last dc worked, ch 6, dc into top of the last dc worked, turn—10 mesh boxes.

**ROW 14:** Ch 9 (counts as ch 3, dc, ch 3), dc in first dc, *ch 3, dc in next dc; rep from * across, sl st down to base of last dc worked, ch 6, dc into the top of the last dc worked, turn—12 mesh boxes.

[Rep Row 2 nine times, then rep Rows 10–14] 4 times, then rep Row 2 nine times.

Fasten off.

## SHELL STRIPS FOR WEAVING
*(make 6 each in B and C)*
See Diagram B at left for sample of patt.

Leave a 6" (15 cm) tail at beg and end of each Shell Strip for sewing ends later.

**ROW 1:** Ch 4 (counts as tr), 3 tr in 4th ch from hook, turn—4 tr.

**ROW 2:** Sl st into each of first 2 sts and into sp before next st, ch 4, 3 tr into same sp, turn.

**ROW 3–72:** Rep Row 2.

Fasten off.

## FINISHING
Lay the mesh scarf out on a table in front of you. Following the Construction Diagram at left, begin weaving one strip in and out through the meshes on the first 9 rows. Rep weaving for all 12 strips.

### Crossing Strips
The next 5 rows of mesh are the point where one color will cross the other. There are five crossings in this scarf. Alternate which color is on top at each crossing point. Starting with one color, weave each of the 6 strips diagonally across the next 6 rows until they are in the columns of the other color strips. Now, with the second color, weave each of the 6 strips diagonally across the same 6 rows until they are in the columns of the other color strips. To secure strips, loosely wrap end of each strip 1–2" (2.5–5 cm) over bottom of mesh panel and using long tail, sew end to itself through a mesh space.

Weave in ends. Handwash, block to finished measurements, and let dry.

## materials

**YARN:** Chunky weight (#5 Bulky), 405 yd (370.3 m).

*Shown:* Tahki, Loop-d-Loop Fern (70% wool, 30% nylon; 81 yd [73 m]/1.75 oz [50 g]): #002 grey-green, 5 balls.

## notions

Tapestry needle

## hook

Q/19 (15mm) or size needed to obtain gauge.

## gauge

About 5 sts = 4" (10 cm) in sc-flo.

## finished size

4" in diameter x 67" long (10 cm x 170.5 cm).

*Wearing a boa* can be so much fun. I used to have a lovely ostrich-feather boa with short downy feathers at the base and luscious long feathers blooming out of the down. I wanted to re-create the look and feel of a feather boa in crochet, with multiple textures for optimal fullness. The super-bulky, textured yarn used in this scarf is perfect because the fur stitch and chain stitches are loose, allowing the yarn's texture to really pop, while the wool base creates a wonderful warmth.

*Harley*

## NOTES

- For instructions on **Fur Stitch (fur st)**, see p. 116.
- Pay close attention to stitch placement on the first few rows, and you'll fly through the rest of the scarf.

*Diagram A*

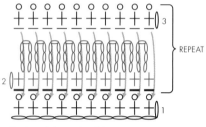

Reduced Sample of Pattern

*Stitch Key*

⬭ = chain (ch)

• = slip st (sl st)

┼ = single crochet (sc)

⚬ over ┼ = fur stitch (fur st)

— = worked in back loop only (blo)

▬ = worked in front loop only (flo)

## SCARF

See Diagram A at left for sample of patt.

Ch 81.

**ROW 1:** Work fur st in 2nd ch from hook and in each ch across, turn—80 sc.

**ROW 2:** Ch 1, sc-flo in first st, *ch 7, sc-flo of next st; rep from * across, turn—79 ch-7 loops.

**ROW 3:** Ch 1, working in rem back loop from Row 1, fur st in each st across, turn—80 sc.

**ROWS 4–9:** Rep Rows 2 and 3 three more times.

**NEXT ROW:** Line up foundation chain and sts from last row together, ch 1, sl st through both thicknesses of each ch and st across. Fasten off; weave in ends.

## FINISHING

Wash, block to finished measurements, and let dry. Fluffing up or gently tugging the loops will make the scarf fuller.

*ivy*

## materials

**YARN:** Worsted weight (#4 Medium), 750 yd (685.8 m).

*Shown:* Caron Simply Soft, Heather (100% acrylic; 250 yd [229 m]/5 oz [142 g]):#9506 deep plum heather, 3 skeins.

## notions

Tapestry needle

## hook

H/8 (5mm) or size needed to obtain gauge.

## gauge

16 sts and 8 rows = 4" (10 cm) in dc.

## finished size

8" wide x 72" long (20.5 cm x 182.9 cm).

*I often draw inspiration* from the ocean and am therefore very partial to wavy (or chevron) stitch patterns. This particular post stitch chevron pattern, while not exactly reversible, is equally as pretty on the right and wrong sides. Ivy is an extra-long scarf because I imagine it wrapped twice around the neck (for double the warmth) with enough left over to drape over the shoulders and down the back. This is the perfect scarf for bundling up to ward off winter gusts.

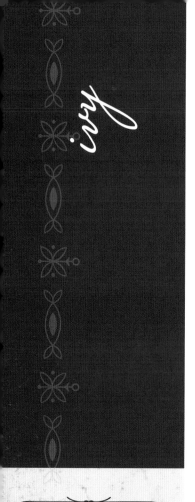

**Diagram A**

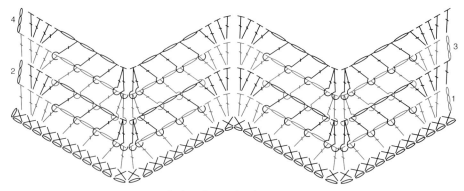

Reduced Sample of Pattern

*Stitch Key*

⬭ = chain (ch)

• = slip st (sl st)

◖X = foundation single crochet (fsc)

† = double crochet (dc)

† = back post double crochet (bpdc)

† = front post double crochet (fpdc)

 = back post cluster (bp-cl)

 = front post cluster (fp-cl)

## NOTES

* For instructions on special stitches used in this pattern, see the following pages: **Foundation Single Crochet (fsc)** p. 115; **Back Post Double Crochet (bpdc)** p. 114; **Back Post Cluster (bp-cl)** p. 114; **Front Post Double Crochet (fpdc)** p. 116; **Front Post Cluster (fp-cl)** p. 116.

* If you are interested in modifying the pattern, please note that the gauge does not reflect the width of the scarf, because a chevron stitch pattern is much narrower than the gauge of the stitches.

## SCARF

See Diagram A above for assistance.

Fsc 42.

**ROW 1 (RS):** Ch 3 (counts as 1st dc), *2 dc in each of next 2 sts, [sk next st, ch 1, dc in next st] 3 times, sk next st, dc in each of next 2 sts, sk next st, [dc in next st, ch 1, sk next st] 3 times, 2 dc in each of next 2 sts; rep from * once more, dc in last st, turn—34 dc and 12 ch-1 sps.

**ROW 2:** Ch 3 (counts as 1st dc), *2 dc in each of next 2 sts, sk next st, [ch 1, bpdc in next dc] 3 times, work bp-cl twice, [bpdc around next st, ch 1] 3 times, sk next st, 2 dc in each of next 2 sts; rep from * once more, dc in last st, turn—18 dcs, 12 bpdc, 4 bp-cl, 12 ch-1 sps.

**ROW 3:** Ch 3 (counts as 1st dc), *2 dc in each of next 2 sts, sk next st, [ch 1, work fpdc around next st] 3 times, work fp-cl twice, [fpdc around next st, ch 1] 3 times, sk next st, 2 dc in each of next 2 sts; rep from * once more, dc in last st, turn—18 dcs, 12 fpdc, 4 fp-cl, 12 ch-1 sps.

Rep Rows 2 and 3 until scarf is 72" (1.8 m) long. Fasten off. Weave in loose ends.

## FINISHING
Wash, block to finished measurements, and let dry.

**VARIATION:** By increasing the width, you can easily modify this pattern to make a shawl. The shawl will require triple the amount of yarn (9 skeins of indicated yarn). To make a shawl 24" wide by 72" (61 cm x 1.8 m) long, triple the width of the scarf, and maintain the length. To work the shawl, fsc 122. Work as for scarf, repeating the pattern across each row a total of six times.

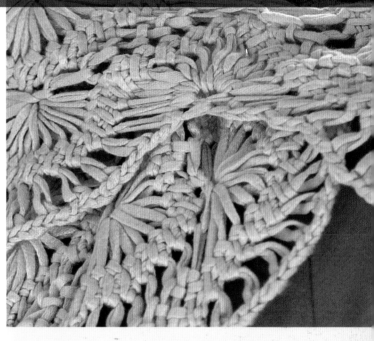

# *Tressa*

## HAIRPIN LACE SCARF

## materials

**YARN:** Worsted weight (#4 Medium), 328 yd (300 m).

*Shown:* Rowan Bamboo Tape (100% bamboo; 82 yd [74.9 m]/1.7 oz [50 g]): #704 lolly, 4 balls.

## tools & notions

Hairpin lace frame, set to 4" (10 cm) wide
Tapestry needle
Split-ring stitch marker

## hook

H/8 (5mm) or size needed to obtain gauge.

## gauge

About 2" wide x 90" long (5 cm x 2.3 m) = 1 strip of hairpin lace. Hairpin lace is very stretchy, so the strips may vary slightly.

## finished size

6" wide x 90" long (15 cm x 2.3 m) without fringe.

*Romantic and delicate,* the Tressa scarf is the perfect accessory to showcase your most beloved ribbon yarn. Ribbon yarns hold a dear place in my heart. I love the look of the yarn, but the texture is mostly lost when you stitch (knit or crochet) with it, so I thought—hairpin lace! Hairpin lace is the perfect expression for this soft and silky ribbon yarn because the pattern highlights the lovely texture. The chevron shaping I used for joining the strips may seem cumbersome at first, but once you get the hang of it you will be delighted with the results!

## HAIRPIN LACE BASICS

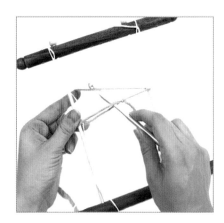

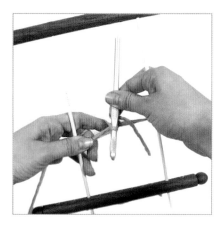

### NOTES

* To keep hairpin lace strips from twisting and tangling once they are removed from the frame, thread waste yarn through the loops on left rod (parallel with left rod) and repeat for the right rod, before taking the strip off of the hairpin lace loom. Waste yarn can also be used once the entire strip is done, and removed from the frame, to bundle all the loops on each side together until you are ready to join another strip.

* When drawing loop through a 15-loop cluster, use a stitch marker to bundle the 15 loops together. It will make it easier to pull the crochet hook and 1 loop through all 15 loops together. Make sure to double check that all 15 loops are secured.

* By alternating the side of the 15-loop cluster (joined with the **Fifteen-to-One Joining** technique on p. 35), you are creating a wavy chevron pattern.

**Step 1. Getting started and making first stitch**

Hold the frame with spacer at bottom and rods 3" (7.5 cm) apart. With yarn, make loop with slipknot and place loop on left rod (counts as first loop), with knot in center between rods. Yarn end wraps from front to back around right rod, and yarn from ball is in front of right rod. Insert hook through loop from bottom to top. Hook yarn and draw through loop.

**Step 2. Moving hook to back, making room for wrapping yarn around loom**

**Drop loop from hook, with hook behind frame. Insert hook from back to front through same loop (just dropped), turn frame clockwise from right to left keeping yarn to back of frame. This allows the yarn to wrap around the frame without the hook getting tangled in the wrap, while retaining the position to continue stitching up the center.

STRIP A

STRIP B

STRIP C

*Joining Diagram*

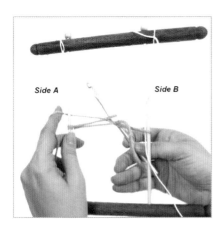

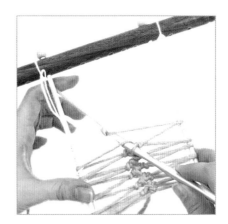

**Step 3. Finish 2nd stitch**

Insert hook under front strand of left loop, yarn over hook, pull loop through. Yarn over hook, pull through 2 loops on hook (single crochet made.**

**Step 4. Continue**

Repeat from ** to ** for desired length of strip. This photo shows what the strip looks like with about 10 stitches complete. Remember: You are crocheting in rows of 1 stitch-per-row vertical crochet.

## STRIP *(make 3)*
Rep Steps 1–4 at left until you have 270 loops wrapped around each of the rods. Fasten off.

## JOINING TWO STRIPS
The loop joining technique joins two strips through one or more loops at a time without any additional yarn. Use your crochet hook to pull the loops through. See Joining Diagram at left for assistance.

### *Fifteen-to-One Joining*
Sk first 7 loops on Strip A (these will be joined later), draw next loop on Strip A through first 15 loops on Strip B (see Notes on page 34).

### One-to-One Joining

Pull next loop on Strip B through loop on hook, pull next loop on Strip A through loop on hook, continue to join loops alternating from B to A until 7 loops on each strip have been individually joined and you have a loop from Strip B on your hook.

Pull loop on hook through next 15 loops on Strip A. Working in the One-to-One Joining technique (as explained above), join the next 7 loops from each strip together. You should have 30 loops from each strip joined together at this point.

*Work in the Fifteen-to-One Joining technique with the next loop on Strip A and next 15 loops on Strip B. Work in the One-to-One Joining technique over the next 7 loops on both strips.

Rep from * 6 more times, alternating which strip gets the 15-loop cluster. You should have 7 free loops rem on Strip B. Tack down the last loop with a tapestry needle and small amount of yarn. Fasten off and weave in ends. Rep technique for joining free loops on Strip B with the loops on Strip C.

### Short Sides of Scarf

Beginning with the first 7 unattached loops on Strip A, insert hook into first loop, *draw next loop through loop on hook; rep from * until 6 loops have been joined and the 7th remains on the hook, draw the first unjoined loop from the bottom side of Strip B through the loop on the hook, draw the next loop through the loop on hook until all loops have been joined, draw the first loop on the bottom side of Strip C through the loop on the hook. Tack down the last loop with a tapestry needle and small amount of yarn and fasten off. Rep technique for joining free loops on the second short side.

### OUTSIDE EDGE OF SCARF (Outer Loops)

Working with crochet hook on free loops of Strip A, join yarn in first loop, *(sc into loop, ch 2) 7 times, sc in next loop, (sc into next loop, ch 2) 7 times, sc15tog over the next 15 loops; rep from * to end, ch 1, work 21 sc evenly along end of 3 joined strips, ch 1, working in free loops of Strip C, **sc in next loop, ch 2, (sc into next loop, ch 2) 7 times, sc15tog over the next 15 loops, (sc into next loop, ch 2) 7 times; rep from ** to end, ch 1, work 21 sc evenly along end of 3 joined strips, join with sl st to first sc at beg of rnd. Fasten off.

## FINISHING

### *Fringe*

Cut 66 strands of fringe, each 14" (35.5 cm) long. Holding 3 strands together, fold fringe in half. Using crochet hook, insert hook from WS to RS into first st along edge, pull folded edge of fringe through to make a loop, insert tail ends into loop and pull tight against edge. Work 11 groups of fringe evenly across each short side of the scarf.

Handwash, block to finished measurements, and let dry.

**THIS CHAPTER CONTAINS A MEDLEY**
of various wrap styles, some of which might
surprise you. A wrap can be so many things,
like a lacy cardi-wrap with sleeves or a cozy
ruana in Tunisian crochet. The projects in this
chapter go far beyond the simple rectangle.
You will find, instead, a wealth of exciting and
unexpected techniques such as a four-color
spiral, infinity motifs, and join-as-you-go strips
of crochet lace to create wraps that will be
treasured for years to come.

# wraps

## materials

**YARN:** Lace weight (#0 Lace), 1,410 yd (1,289.3 m).

*Shown:* Malabrigo Merino Lace (100% baby merino; 470 yd [429.7 m]/1.75 oz [50 g]): #137 emerald blue, 3 skeins.

## notions

Tapestry needle
Split-ring stitch markers

## hook

G/6 (4mm) or size needed to obtain gauge.

## gauge

20 sts and 8 rows = 4" (10 cm) in dc.

## finished size

20" wide x 98" long (51 cm x 233.7 cm).

*I lived on the Mediterranean*
Sea for several years and had the distinct pleasure of viewing emerald and sapphire seas every day. The infinity motifs in this wrap remind me of the swirling tides of the water, while the color of the yarn brings back wonderful memories of the sea. This versatile piece can be worn as a scarf, wrapped around your neck several times. It is also wide enough to drape across your back as a wrap. Try wrapping it around from back to front, cross the ends over your chest, and tie them in the back for a pretty capelet look.

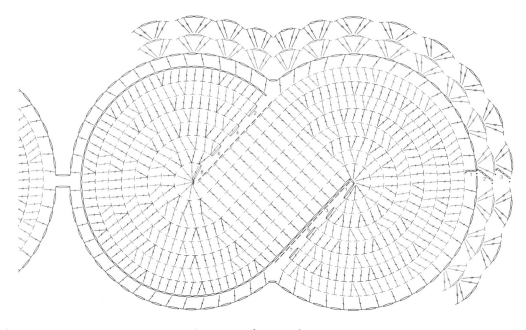

Infinity Motif

## NOTES

▪ The center motifs are worked in rows. Once the center motif is created and sewn into shape the lace border is worked in the round, picking up and joining motifs as you go.

▪ There are a lot of concentrated increases worked into Round 1 when joining motifs. Don't be concerned if the garment appears overly ruffled on the first couple of rounds. Even after all rounds are completed, the scarf will have a ruffled outer edge.

▪ Do not remove markers in joining round until the entire round is completed.

### *Stitch Key*

⬭ = chain (ch)

• = slip st (sl st)

⊤ = double crochet (dc)

⊤ = treble crochet (tr)

## WRAP

See Diagram A above for assistance.

### MOTIF *(Make 5)*

Ch 76 very loosely.

**ROW 1:** 8 dc in second ch from hook, dc in each of next 10 ch, [dc in next ch, dc2tog, dc in each of next 5 ch] 8 times, turn—74 sts.

**RND 2:** Sl st into first ch-1 sp, ch 4 (counts as tr), (tr, ch 2, 2 tr) in same sp, (2 tr, ch 2, 2 tr) in each ch-1 sp around, join with sl st in top of ch-4.

**RND 3:** Sl st into first ch-2 sp, ch 4 (counts as tr), (tr, ch 2, 2 tr) in same sp, (2 tr, ch 2, 2 tr) in each ch-2 sp around, join with sl st in top of ch-4.

**RNDS 4–8:** Rep Rnd 3.

## MOTIF FINISHING

Using Diagram A at left as a guide, sew end of rows to each side of center 10 sts. There should be 64 sts rem unattached on each rounded side of motif. Pm in center st of each rounded end for placement of joining row.

### *Joining Motifs*

RND 1: Beg with one side of first motif, join yarn with sl st in same st as marker, ch 4 (counts as dc, ch 1), sk next st, *(dc, ch 1) in next st, sk next st; rep from * to pm at opposite end, (dc, ch 1) in marked st. Pick up 2nd motif, (dc, ch 1) in first marked st of 2nd motif, sk next st, rep from * to pm at opposite end of 2nd motif, (dc, ch 1) in marked st. Work 3rd, 4th, and 5th motifs as for 2nd. Continuing around opposite side of motifs, work in est patt to each marked st of all motifs, join with sl st to 3rd ch of beg ch-4—320 ch-1 sps.

RND 2: Sl st into first ch-1 sp, ch 4 (counts as tr), (tr, ch 2, 2 tr) in same sp, (2 tr, ch 2, 2 tr) in each ch-1 sp around, join with sl st in top of ch-4.

RND 3: Sl st into first ch-2 sp, ch 4 (counts as tr), (tr, ch 2, 2 tr) in same sp, (2 tr, ch 2, 2 tr) in each ch-2 sp around, join with sl st in top of ch-4.

RNDS 4–8: Rep Rnd 3.

Fasten off and weave in ends.

## FINISHING

Handwash, block to measurements, and let dry.

*zeena*

## materials

**YARN:** Chunky weight (#5 Bulky), 1,001 yd (915.3 m) A; 429 yd (392.3 m) B—1,144 yd (1,046 m) total.

*Shown:* Plymouth Yarns, Encore Chunky (75% acrylic, 25% wool; 143 yd [131 m]/3.5 oz [100 g]): chocolate (A), 9 balls; teal (B), 3 balls.

## notions

Tapestry needle

## hook

M/9mm Tunisian hook and K/10.5 (6.5mm) crochet hook or size needed to obtain gauge.

## gauge

10 sts and 9½ rows = 4" (10 cm) with Tunisian hook and working in Tunisian Simple Stitch (Tss).

## finished size

34½" wide x 33" long (87.5 cm x 84 cm) at the back. Each front panel is 16" (40.5 cm) wide.

*There comes a time of year* when it's too cold for just a cardigan, but it's not quite time to pull out your winter coat. It is the perfect time to snuggle into this ruana-style wrap. The Tunisian stitch pattern is quite dense and is worked in two colors, resulting in a fabric with an interesting woven look. A versatile piece, Zeena is easy to throw on while retaining a structured look. It can be worn open, cinched with a belt, or even with one side slung over a shoulder.

## TUNISIAN SIMPLE STITCH (Tss)

- **Row 1 (forward row):** Chain number of stitches indicated in pattern, insert hook in second chain from hook, yarn over hook, pull up loop, *insert hook in next chain, yarn over hook, pull up loop; repeat from * across, leaving all loops on hook. Do not turn.

- **(Return row):** To complete row, work loops off hook as follows: yarn over hook, pull through 1 loop on hook, *yarn over hook, pull through 2 loops on hook; repeat from * across, until 1 loop remains on hook (counts as first stitch of next row).

- **Row 2 (forward row):** Skip first vertical bar, insert hook under next vertical bar, yarn over hook, pull up loop, *insert hook under next vertical bar, yarn over hook, pull up loop; repeat from * across. Do not turn.

- **(Return row):** To complete row, work loops off as follows: yarn over hook, pull through 1 loop on hook, *yarn over hook, pull through 2 loops on hook; repeat from * across, until 1 loop remains on hook (counts as first stitch of next row).

### Diagram A

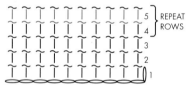

Reduced Sample of Pattern

### Stitch Key

- ⬯ = chain (ch)
- | = Tunisian simple stitch (Tss) first half of row
- ～ = Tunisian simple stitch (Tss) second half of row
- ■ = color A
- ■ = color B

### WRAP

See Diagram A at left for sample of patt.

### RIGHT FRONT

With A and Tunisian hook, ch 40.

**ROW 1:** Work Row 1 of Tss—40 sts.

**ROWS 2–3:** Work Row 2 of Tss.

**ROW 4:** Continue in Tss, working forward row with A, drop A to RS of work, change to B for return row.

**ROW 5:** Continue in patt, working forward row with B, drop B to RS of work, change to A for return row.

**ROWS 6–32:** Rep Rows 4 and 5 thirteen more times. Fasten off B.

**ROWS 33–79:** With A, work in Tss. Fasten off.

### BACK NECK

With A, ch 6 and fasten off. This piece will be used to join the right front and left front pieces.

## LEFT FRONT

Work as for Right Front, but don't fasten off.

## BACK

**ROW 1:** With RS facing, work forward row of Tss across Left Front, insert hook in 1st ch of ch-6 piece, yo, pull up loop, *insert hook in next ch of ch-6 piece, yo, pull up loop; rep from * to end of ch-6 piece, working across last row of Right Front, with RS facing, insert hook under first vertical bar, yo, pull up loop, *insert hook under next vertical bar, yo, pull up a loop; rep from * across right front—86 loops on hook. Work return row.

**ROW 2–48:** Work Row 2 of Tss.

**ROW 49–76:** Work Rows 4 and 5 of Right Front 14 times.

**ROW 77–79:** Work Row 2 of Tss. Fasten off.

## FINISHING

With regular crochet hook and RS facing, join A with sl st to center of lower back in a vertical bar, ch 1, sc in same vertical bar. Work 1 sc in each vertical bar to end of row, 3 sc in corner sp, work 1 sc in end of every row along to next corner, 3 sc in corner sp, sc in each beg chain across bottom of Right Front, 3 sc in corner sp, work 1 sc in each end of row along to neck, sc in each beg ch of Back Neck, work 1 sc in each end of row along to next corner, 3 sc in corner sp, sc in each beg ch of Left Front, 3 sc in corner sp, work 1 sc in each end of row across to next corner, 3 sc in corner, work 1 sc in each vertical bar to beg of rnd, join with sl st to first sc at beg of rnd. Fasten off.

Wash, block to finished measurements, and let dry.

# ayla

## materials

**YARN:** DK weight (#3 Light), 900 (1,050, 1,200) yd (823 [960.1, 1,097.3] m) A; 360 (420, 480) yd (329.2 [384, 438.9] m) B; 180 (210, 240) yd (164.6 [192, 219.5] m) each C and D—1,620 (1,890, 2,160) yd (1,481.3 [1,728.2, 1,975.1] m) total.

*Shown:* Naturally Naturelle 8 ply (100% wool; 210 yd [192 m]/3.5 oz [100 g]): #151 ash (A), 5 (5, 7) balls; #152 sable (B), 2 (2, 3) balls; #154 charcoal (C), 1 (1, 2) ball; #160 navy (D), 1 (1, 2) ball.

## notions

Tapestry needle
Split-ring stitch markers

## hook

H/8 (5mm) or size needed to obtain gauge.

## gauge

12 sts and 6 rows = 4" (10 cm) in dc and 12 sts and 10 rows = 4" (10 cm) in hdc-blo.

## finished size

Sized to fit 30 (35, 40)" (76 [89, 102] cm) bust with 20" (51 cm) long sleeves. This wrap is meant to fit loosely.

*This wrap was inspired* by a strong and rugged character in a novel I read. I imagine wearing this piece as you are hiking through the mountains on a cold but sunny afternoon. The wool is warm and rustic, and you can wrap the garment tightly to protect you from the whipping winds. The spiral featured on the back works with the circular hem and bell sleeves to create a unique wrap that provides both comfort and style.

*Diagram A—Size Small*

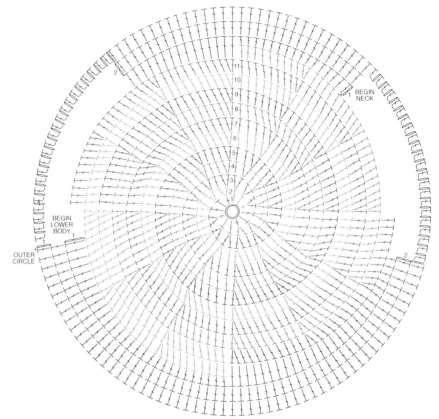

## NOTES

- For instructions on **Puff Stitch (puff st),** see p. 117.

- For instructions on **Foundation Double Crochet (fdc),** see p. 116.

- When you drop a color, remove the hook from the loop, then place a stitch marker in the loop to reserve it for later.

- Turning chain does not count as a stitch unless otherwise directed.

## SWIRL

See Diagram A according to your size for assistance.

**RND 1:** With A, make an adjustable ring, ch 1, work (sc, hdc, dc) into ring, drop A (see Notes p. 50), *join B, ch 1, work (sc, hdc, dc) into adjustable ring, drop B; rep from * with C and then D, do not drop D. Tighten adjustable ring to close "circle" with 4 sections of different colors—3 sts of each color, 12 sts total.

*Note:* Pm in last st of D to denote beg of rnd, move pm with the beg of each rnd.

**RND 2:** With D, 2 dc in each of next 3 sts, *drop D and pick up reserved loop of color A; work 2 dc in each of next 3 sts; rep from * with rem colors for rnd, do not drop C—24 sts.

**RND 3:** With C, *[2 dc next st, dc in next st] 3 times; rep from * with each of D, A, and B, do not drop B—36 sts.

**RND 4:** With B, *[2 dc in next st, dc in each of next 2 sts] 3 times; rep from * with each of C, D, and A, do not drop A—48 sts.

**RND 5:** With A, *[2 dc in next st, dc in each of next 3 sts] 3 times; rep from * with each of B, C, and D, do not drop D—60 sts.

*Note:* You will be inc 12 sts per rnd in est patt working 3 inc per color section per rnd.

**RNDS 6–11 (13, 14):** Continue in est patt until you have 33 (39, 42) sts in each color section—132 (156, 168) sts total.

Fasten off all sts.

*Diagram A—Size Medium*

*Diagram A—Size Large*

**Stitch Key**

◯ = chain (ch)

• = slip st (sl st)

✝ = single crochet (sc)

T = half double crochet (hdc)

T = double crochet (dc)

= foundation double crochet (fdc)

= shell (sh)

= puff st

**Schematic**

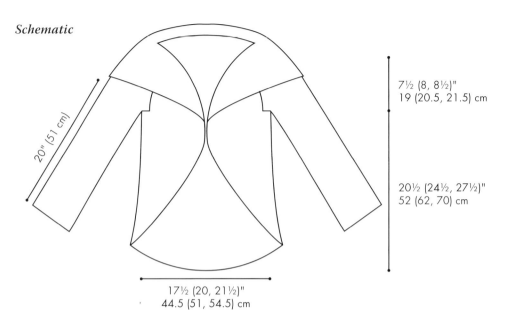

7½ (8, 8½)"
19 (20.5, 21.5) cm

20" (51 cm)

20½ (24½, 27½)"
52 (62, 70) cm

17½ (20, 21½)"
44.5 (51, 54.5) cm

## SET UP FOR BODY AND SLEEVE OPENINGS

### Begin Neck

ROW 1: With A and RS facing, join with sl st in any st, ch 2, dc in same st and in each of next 30 (38, 44) sts, turn.

ROW 2: Ch 2, dc in same st and in each of next 30 (38, 44) sts across—31 (39, 45) dc.

Fasten off.

### Begin Lower Body

ROW 1: With RS facing, sk next 22 (24, 26) sts of Swirl Rnd 11 (13, 14) join A with sl st to next st, ch 2, dc in same st and in each of next 56 (68, 70) sts, turn.

ROW 2: Ch 2, dc in same st and in each st across, turn, do not fasten off, continue on to outer circle.

## OUTER CIRCLE

See Diagram B on p. 53 for assistance.

RND 1: With RS facing, ch 2, dc in same st and in each of next 56 (68, 70) sts, work 22 (24, 26) fdc, sk next 22 (24, 26) sts of Swirl Rnd 11 (13, 14), dc in each of next 31 (39, 45) sts, work 22 (24, 26) fdc, sk next 22 (24, 26) sts of Swirl Rnd 11 (13, 14), join with sl st to beg dc—132 (156, 168) dc.

*Note:* On next rnd, we will be doubling the stitches. This allows us to work in the round over the next several rows without having to increase the stitch pattern.

RND 2: Ch 3 (counts as dc), 3 dc in first st (counts as first 4-dc), skip next st, *4-dc in next st, sk next st; rep from * around, sl st in first dc to join—66 (78, 84) 4-dc.

Fasten off.

RND 3: Join C with sl st in sp bet any two 4-dc, ch 2, puff st in same sp, *ch 4, skip next 4-dc, puff st in sp bet next two 4-dc; rep from * around, ch 4, sl st to top of first puff st. Fasten off.

RND 4: Join B with sl st in any ch-4 sp, ch 3 (counts as dc), 3 dc in same sp, *4-dc in next ch-4 sp; rep from * around, join with sl st to first dc. Fasten off.

RND 5: With D, rep Rnd 3. Fasten off.

RND 6: With A, rep Rnd 4. Fasten off.

Rep Rnds 3–6 two (three, four) more times.

*Diagram B*

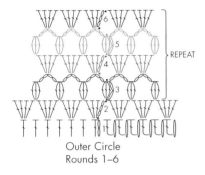

Outer Circle
Rounds 1–6

## SLEEVES

Beg with one sleeve, join A with sl st in center st at underarm, ch 2, hdc in each st around sleeve opening, sl st in first hdc to join.

**ROW 1:** Ch 62, turn, hdc in 3rd ch from hook, and in each ch across, sl st into next 2 sts from sleeve opening, turn.

**ROW 2:** Hdc-blo in each st across, turn—60 hdc.

**ROW 3:** Ch 2, hdc-blo in each st across, sl st into next 2 sts from sleeve opening, turn.

Rep Rows 2 and 3 until you have placed a sl st in each st of sleeve opening. Fasten off.

### *Seam Sleeve*

Holding RS together and working through both thicknesses, join A and sc ch edge and last row worked of sleeve together. Fasten off and weave in tails. Rep for second sleeve.

## FINISHING

Handwash, block to schematic dimensions, above, and let dry. Sew buttons, attach a toggle to the front, use a shawl pin, or cinch a belt around the wrap for closure. Or you can just let the wrap fall naturally.

# prima ballerina

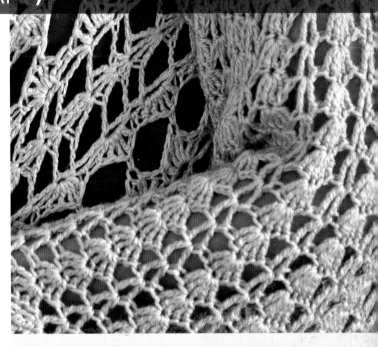

## materials

**YARN:** Dk weight (#3 Light), 1,400 yd (1,280.2 m).

*Shown:* Blue Sky Alpacas, Alpaca Silk (50% alpaca, 50% silk; 146 yd [133 m]/ 1.75 oz [50 g]): #114 wisteria, 10 (12, 13, 14) skeins.

## notions

Removable stitch markers
Tapestry needle

## hook

G/6 (4mm) or size needed to obtain gauge.

## gauge

First 6 rows of strip = 2½" wide x 4½" long (6.5 cm x 11.5 cm). Each strip is 4¼" wide x 63 (68, 72, 77)" long (11.5 cm x 160 [172, 184, 196] cm), including border.

## finished size

Sized to fit 30 (34, 38, 42)" (76 [86, 97, 107] cm) bust; 21" (53.5 cm) long.

*This rectangular wrap* with long, belled sleeves (also known as a cardi-wrap) brings to mind the graceful elegance of a ballerina. Wear it open, tied, or even wrapped in front and secured with a beautiful shawl pin to add flair to an evening outfit. The feminine lace details and delicate scalloped edge add to the luxurious drape of the alpaca-and-silk blend yarn.

**Diagram A**

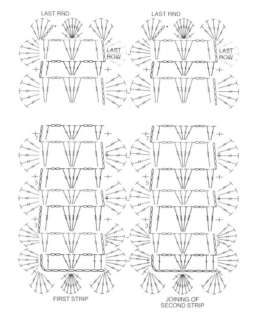

FIRST STRIP

JOINING OF
SECOND STRIP

**Diagram B**

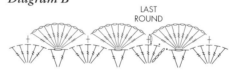

LAST
ROUND

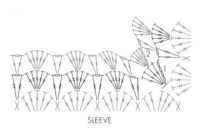

SLEEVE

**Stitch Key**

$\frown$ = chain (ch)

• = slip stitch (sl st)

+ = single crochet (sc)

= double crochet (dc)

= treble crochet (tr)

= double treble
    crochet (dtr)

## NOTE

This wrap is crocheted in 4"
(10 cm) wide strips that are
joined as you go. The sleeve
openings are made by simply
skipping a few inches of the
joining of the strips. The
sleeves are picked up from the
openings and worked in the
round seamlessly.

**Schematic**

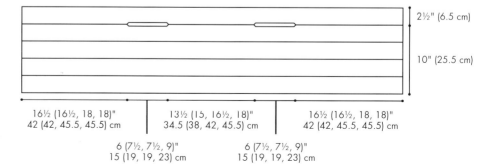

2½" (6.5 cm)

10" (25.5 cm)

16½ (16½, 18, 18)"
42 (42, 45.5, 45.5) cm

13½ (15, 16½, 18)"
34.5 (38, 42, 45.5) cm

16½ (16½, 18, 18)"
42 (42, 45.5, 45.5) cm

6 (7½, 7½, 9)"
15 (19, 19, 23) cm

6 (7½, 7½, 9)"
15 (19, 19, 23) cm

## STRIPS *(make 5)*

See Diagram A at left for assistance.

Ch 11 loosely.

**ROW 1:** Sk first 3 ch (counts as dc), dc in 4th ch from hook, sk 2 ch, ch 2, 4 dc in next ch, sk 2 ch, ch 2, dc in each of last 2 ch, turn—8 dc.

**ROW 2:** Ch 4 (counts as tr), sk 1st dc, tr in sp before next dc, ch 2, sk next 3 dc, 4 tr in sp before next dc, ch 2, sk next 3 dc, 2 tr in sp before last dc, turn—8 tr.

**ROW 3:** Ch 5 (counts as dtr), sk 1st tr, dtr in sp before next tr, ch 2, sk next 3 tr, 4 dtr in sp before next tr, ch 2, sk next 3 tr, 2 dtr in sp before last tr, turn—8 dtr.

**ROW 4:** Ch 3 (counts as dc), sk 1st dtr, dc in sp before next dtr, ch 2, sk next 3 dtr, 4 dc in sp before next dtr, ch 2, sk next 3 dtr, 2 dc in sp before last dtr, turn.

Rep Rows 2–4 twenty-five (twenty-seven, twenty-nine, thirty-one) more times, then Row 2 once more.

## JOINING STRIPS

See Diagram A on p. 56 for assistance.

Finish first strip with one last rnd. Rem strips will be joined to each other in the last rnd as follows:

### First Strip Only

**LAST RND:** Turn work clockwise 90 degrees so you are working across the long edge, ch 4 (counts as tr), work (4 tr, sc, 5 tr) in end of last st worked in prev row, *[sc in next end of row, 5 tr in next end of row (scallop made]] across to last end of row, (5 tr, sc, 5 tr) in last end of row, turn work 90 degrees and work (sc, 7 tr, sc) in centermost ch of short edge*, turn work 90 degrees, work (5tr, sc, 5 tr) in first end of row, rep from * to * once, join with sl st to top of beg tr. Fasten off.

### Join Second Strip to First Strip

**JOINING RND:** Turn work clockwise 90 degrees so you are working across the long edge, ch 4 (counts as tr), work (4 tr, sc, 3 tr, sl st into corresponding 3rd tr in first strip, 2 tr) all in end of last st worked in prev row, *[sc in next end of row, (3 tr, sl st into corresponding 3rd tr in first strip, 2 tr) in next end of row] across to last end of row, work (3 tr, sl st in corresponding tr on first strip, 2 tr, sc, 5 tr) all in last row end, turn work 90 degrees, work (sc, 7 tr, sc) in centermost ch on short edge*, turn work 90 degrees, work (5 tr, sc, 5 tr) in first end of row; rep from * to * once, join with sl st to top of first tr. Fasten off.

Rep Joining Rnd to join 3rd strip to 2nd strip and 4th strip to 3rd strip.

When joining 5th strip to 4th strip, the armhole openings are made on Joining Rnd as follows: Turn work clockwise 90 degrees to work across long edge, ch 4 (counts as tr), work (4 tr, sc, 3 tr, sl st into corresponding 3rd tr in adjacent strip, 2 tr) all in first row end, *[sc in next end of row, work (3 tr, sl st into corresponding 3rd tr in adjacent strip, 2 tr) in next end of row]* 11 (11, 12, 12) times, pm around last sl st joining strips, **[sc in next end of row, 5 tr in next end of row] 4 (5, 5, 6) times**, rep from * to * 9 (10, 11, 12) times, pm around last sl st joining strips, rep from ** to **, rep from * to * 11 (11, 12, 12) times, work (3 tr, sl st in corresponding 3rd tr in adjacent strip, 2 tr, sc, 5 tr) all in last row end, turn work clockwise 90 degrees and finish Joining Rnd as for previous strips.

## SLEEVES

See Diagram B on p. 56 for assistance.

Working around sleeve opening on wrap, join yarn with sl st in first marker, ch 4 (counts as tr), 4 tr into same sp, (dtr, ch 1, dtr) into next sc on strip, *5 tr into 3rd tr of next scallop, (dtr, ch 1, dtr) into next sc*, rep from * to * 3 (4, 4, 5) more times, work 5 tr into next sl st sp joining strips, (dtr, ch 1, dtr) into next sc on next strip, rep from * to * 4 (5, 5, 6) times, join with sl st to top of ch-4 at beg of rnd.

**RND 2:** Sl st into each of next 2 sts, ch 4 (counts as tr), 4 tr into same st, (tr, ch 1, tr) into next ch-1 sp, *5 tr into 3rd tr of next scallop, (tr, ch 1, tr) into next ch-1 sp; rep from * around, join with sl st to top of beg ch-4.

Rep Rnd 2 until piece measures 20" (51 cm) from beg of sleeve.

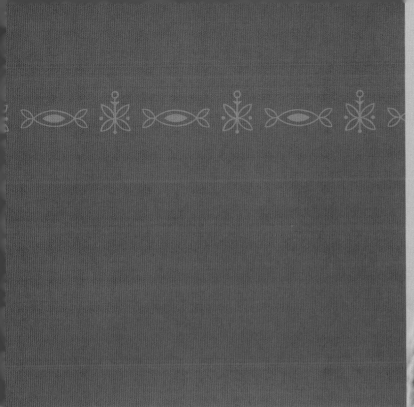

**LAST RND:** Sl st into each of next 2 sts, ch 1, sc in first st, ([dtr, ch 1] 8 times, dtr) in next ch-1 sp, *sc in 3rd tr of next scallop, ([dtr, ch 1] 8 times, dtr) in next ch-1 sp; rep from * around, join with sl st to first sc. Fasten off.

Work second sleeve as for first.

## FINISHING

Handwash, block to finished measurements, and let dry. Weave in loose ends.

**VARIATION:** If you want to make this a rectangular wrap without sleeves, just follow the instructions for joining the first and second strips until you have 5 strips joined. It will take 760 yd (694.9 m) of yarn. Weave in loose ends, block to finished measurements, and let dry.

*geisha*

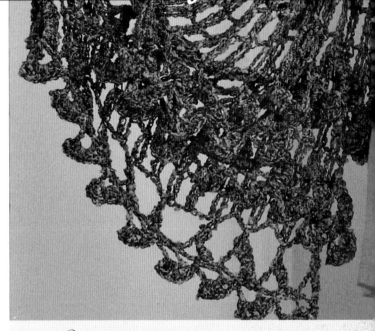

## materials

**YARN:** Worsted weight (#4 Medium), 820 yd (749.8 m).

*Shown:* Filatura di Crosa, Ariel (50% cotton, 40% viscose, 10% polyamide; 164 yd [149 m]/1.75 oz [50 g]): pink peach #7, 5 balls.

## notions

Tapestry needle

## hook

I/9 (5.5mm) or size needed to obtain gauge.

## gauge

14 sts and 8 rows = 4" (10 cm) in stitch pattern.

## finished size

68" wide x 20" long (51 cm x 172.7 cm).

*I chose an ultra-simple stitch pattern for this wrap to showcase the wonderful texture of the yarn, rather than the texture of the stitches. The majority of the shawl is simply chains! The simple, linear construction of the stitch pattern also made it a perfect candidate for tiers of edging, joined as you go. This particular edging appealed to me because it reminded me of a Japanese geisha fan. This edging also worked well because the distance between the two-row repeats matched perfectly for joining to the shawl at every fourth row.*

*geisha*

## Diagram A

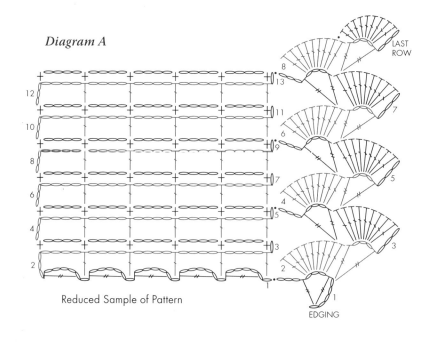

Reduced Sample of Pattern

### Stitch Key

$\bigcirc$ = chain (ch)

$\bullet$ = slip stitch (sl st)

$+$ = single crochet (sc)

$\dagger$ = double crochet (dc)

$\ddagger$ = treble crochet (tr)

## NOTES

■ For instructions on **V Stitch (v-st),** see p. 117.

■ Edging is joined to the body of the shawl as you go.

## WRAP

See Diagram A above for assistance.

**ROW 1 (RS):** *Ch 6, tr in 5th ch from hook; rep from * 48 more times—49 ch-4 loops.

**ROW 2:** Ch 7 (counts as dc, ch-4), sk first ch-4 loop, dc in next ch, *ch 4, sk next ch-4 loop, dc in next ch; rep from * across—49 ch-4 sps.

**ROW 3:** Ch 1, sc in 1st dc, *ch 4, sk next ch-4 sp, sc in next dc; rep from * across.

**ROW 4:** Ch 7 (counts as dc, ch-4), sk first ch-4 sp, dc in next sc, *ch 4, sk next ch-4 sp, dc in next sc; rep from * across.

**ROW 5:** Rep Row 3.

**ROWS 6–41:** Rep Rows 4 and 5. Fasten off.

## EDGING

Ch 5.

**ROW 1:** V-st in 5th ch from hook, ch 3, with RS facing and shawl laying horizontally in front of you, sl st in lower right hand corner of shawl (see Diagram A at left) to join, turn.

**ROW 2:** Sk first ch-3 sp, 9 dc into ch-3 sp of v-st from prev edging row, skip next tr, v-st into ch-5 sp, turn.

**ROW 3:** Ch 3, 9 dc into ch-3 sp, sk next tr, v-st in sp bet next two dc, ch 3, skip first 4 rows of shawl, sl st in ch-1 sp of next row of shawl to join, turn.

**ROW 4:** Sk first ch-3 sp, 9 dc into ch-3 sp of v-st, skip next tr, v-st in sp bet next two dc, turn.

**ROW 5:** Ch 3, 9 dc into ch-3 sp, sk next tr, v-st in sp bet next two dc, ch 3, sk next 3 rows of wrap, sl st in ch-1 sp at beg of next row, turn.

Rep Rows 4 and 5 eight times, then rep Row 4 once more.

**LAST ROW:** Ch 3, 9 dc into ch-3 sp, sk next tr, sl st in sp bet next 2 dc. Fasten off.

With RS facing, rotate shawl and rep Edging rows for opposite side.

With RS facing, rep all Edging rows at 4" (10 cm) and again at 8½" (21.5 cm) in from each short end, joining the Edging to the body of the shawl by working joining sl st around sc posts instead of the ch-1 sp.

## FINISHING

Handwash, block to finished measurements, and let dry.

I LOVE SHAWLS! I love to design them, wear them, and give them as gifts. They can be sexy, warm, comforting, elegant, outrageous—sometimes all at once. A classic part of a woman's wardrobe, shawls are easy to wear and add a distinctly feminine touch to any outfit. In the following chapter, you will find a variety of styles, each exploring different techniques, patterns, and silhouettes. You will find a casual shawl in soft, warm wool for a chilly afternoon, a slinky, sequined silk mesh confection for a night on the town, and everything in between.

# shawls

*guinevere*

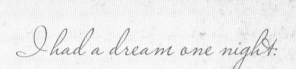

## materials

**YARN:** Sportweight (#2 Fine), 1,350 yd (1,234 4 m).

*Shown:* Muench Yarn GGH, Soft Kid (70% super kid mohair, 25% polymid, 5% new wool; 151 yd [138 m]/1 oz [25 g]): # 37 raspberry, 9 balls.

## notions

Size 17 (12.75 mm) knitting needle
Tapestry needle
Split-ring stitch markers

## hook

I/9 (5.5mm) or size needed to obtain gauge.

## gauge

4 repeats and 6 rows = 4" (10 cm) in mesh triangle patt.

24 sts and 8 rows = 4" (10 cm) in broomstick lace patt.

## finished size

72" wide x 32" long (182.9 cm x 31.5 cm).

*I had a dream one night:*

I envisioned the center panel of a beautiful shawl made of crocheted broomstick lace in a gorgeous mohair yarn. I remembered the fiber's halo catching natural sunlight through a window. Thus Guinevere was born! The shoulder shaping is achieved with a gusset that allows the shawl to stay on your shoulders whether you tie it, pin it, or simply let it hang loose!

*Diagram A*

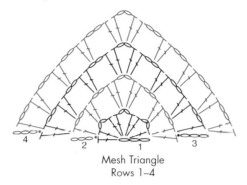

Mesh Triangle
Rows 1–4

*Diagram B*

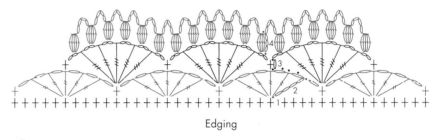

Edging

*Diagram C*

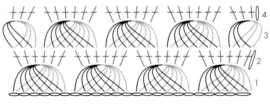

Reduced Sample of Broomstick Lace Pattern

## NOTES

* For instructions on special stitches used in this pattern see the following pages: **Broomstick Lace Pattern (broomstick lace patt)** p. 114; **Shell (sh)** p. 117; **4 Double Crochet Bobble (4-dc bobble)** p. 115; **5 Double Crochet Bobble (5-dc bobble)** p. 115.

* Broomstick lace is not turned. The side facing you is the right side. The first row of broomstick lace is worked from left to right. The second row is worked from right to left.

* When pulling up loops for first row of broomstick lace, be sure that the loops don't get twisted when placed on the needle.

*Stitch Key*

| | |
|---|---|
| ⬭ | = chain (ch) |
| • | = slip stitch (sl st) |
| + | = single crochet (sc) |
| ┬ | = double crochet (dc) |
| ‡ | = treble crochet (tr) |
| ‡ | = double treble crochet (dtr) |
| ⬮ | = 4-dc bobble |
| ⬮ | = 5-dc bobble |

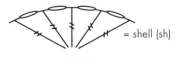 = shell (sh)

 = 3 loops of broomstick lace

## GUSSET

Ch 60, turn ch so last loop worked is on the left.

**ROW 1:** Using hook, pull the last ch worked up long enough to place onto knitting needle and remove hook, *insert hook into next ch, yo and pull up a loop long enough to place onto knitting needle, remove hook; rep from * across—60 loops on knitting needle.

**ROWS 2–20:** Beg with Row 2, work in broomstick lace patt.

**ROW 21:** Sk 1st st, working from left to right, sl st into each of next 3 sts, place loop onto knitting needle, remove hook; *insert hook into next ch, pull up a loop and place onto knitting needle, remove hook; rep from * across to last 3 sts, leave rem 3 sts unworked—54 loops.

**ROW 22:** Work Row 2 of broomstick lace patt.

**ROW 23:** Rep Row 21—48 loops.

**ROW 24:** Work Row 4 of broomstick lace patt.

**ROW 25:** Rep Row 21—42 loops.

Rep Rows 22–25 three times, then rep Row 2 once more—6 sc. Fasten off.

## MESH TRIANGLE *(make 2)*

See Diagram A at left for assistance.

**ROW 1:** Ch 3 (counts as dc here and throughout patt), (dc, [ch 2, 2 dc] 3 times) in 3rd ch from hook, turn—8 dc, 3 ch-2 sps.

**ROW 2:** Sl st into sp bet 1st and 2nd dc, ch 3, dc in same sp, *ch 2, 2 dc in next ch-2 sp*, ch 2, (2 dc, ch 2, 2 dc) in next ch-2 sp, rep from* to * once, ch 2, 2 dc bet last 2 dc, turn—5 ch-2 sps.

**ROW 3:** Sl st into sp bet 1st and 2nd dc, ch 3, dc in same sp, *ch 2, 2 dc in next ch-2 sp*, rep from * to * once more, ch 2, (2 dc, ch 2, 2 dc) in next ch-2 sp, rep from * to * twice, ch 2, 2 dc bet last 2 dc, turn—7 ch-2 sps.

**ROWS 4–27:** Rep as est in Row 3, inc each row by 2 ch-2 sps—55 ch-2 sps.

Fasten off and weave in ends.

## Schematic

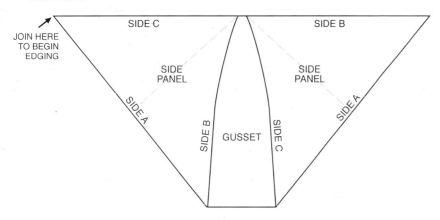

JOIN HERE
TO BEGIN
EDGING

SIDE C

SIDE B

SIDE
PANEL

SIDE
PANEL

SIDE A

SIDE A

SIDE B

SIDE C

GUSSET

## SEW GUSSET AND
## SIDE PANELS TOGETHER

Lightly spray-block each piece before sewing together, blocking each piece so shorter sides of triangles are equal to sides of gusset.

Sew the center gusset panel to the side triangles, following the schematic at left. Note that the widest side of the triangle is where you started (Side A), this side forms the bottom "V" of the large, triangular shawl. Sides B and C are the same length.

## EDGING

See Diagram B on p. 68 for assistance.

Edging is worked in the round with RS facing.

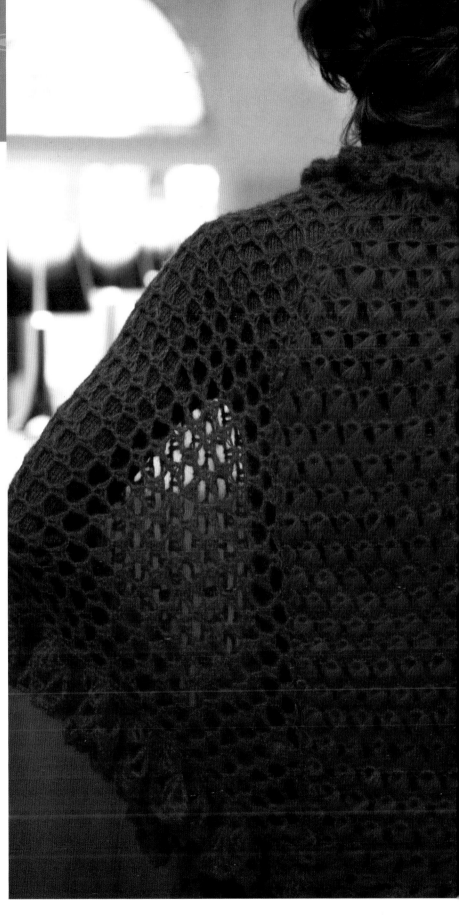

**RND 1:** With RS facing and working along bottom "V" edge of shawl, join yarn in upper left corner, work 6 sc into end of each dc row of Side A—162 sc; 2 sc into each free loop of beg ch from the center gusset—120 sc; 6 sc into each dc end of each dc row of the second Side A—162 sc; turn to work along top edge, 4 sc into each ch-2 sp across top right of shawl—108 sc; sc into each sc of top row of broomstick Gusset, 4 sc into each ch-2 sp across top left of shawl—108 sc; join with sl st to first sc at beg of round—660 sc.

**RND 2:** Ch 5, [tr, ch 1] 4 times in same sp (counts as first sh), sk next 4 sts, sc in next st, ch 1, sk next 4 sts, *sh in next st, sk next 4 sts, sc in next st, ch 1, sk next 4 sts; rep from * around, sl st to 4th ch of beg ch-5 to join rnd.

**RND 3:** Sl st across to center tr of first sh, ch 1, sc in same st, *ch 2, [dtr, ch 2] 5 times in next sc, sc into center tr of next sh; rep from * around, sl st to first sc at beg of rnd to join.

**RND 4:** Sl st into first ch-2 sp, ch 3, 4-dc bobble in same sp, *ch 4, 5-dc bobble in next ch-2 sp; rep from * around, ch 4, sl st into top of ch-4 bobble at beg of rnd to join.

## FINISHING
Handwash, block to finished measurements, and let dry. Weave in loose ends.

# MEDALLION TRIANGULAR SHAWL

## materials

**YARN:** DK weight (#3 Light), 950 yd (868.7 m).

*Shown:* Patons Grace, (100% mercerized cotton; 136 yd [125 m]/1.7 oz [50 g]): #60011 champagne, 7 balls.

## notions

Tapestry needle

## hook

F/5 (3.75mm) and H/8 (5mm) or sizes needed to obtain gauge.

## gauge

16 sts and 8 rows = 4" (10 cm) in hdc-blo with larger hook. Motif = 7½" (19 cm) in diameter with smaller hook.

## finished size

72" wide x 44" long (1.8 m x 112 cm).

*Long before I began* designing shawls, I came across a famous Italian designer's crocheted shawl with circular motifs along the bottom edge of the otherwise simple mesh triangular shawl. I fell in love with the relationship of simplicity to complexity in the shawl and created my own interpretation of the concept in the Maya shawl. The body of the shawl features half double crochet through the back loops, leaving a lovely, sharp, linear detail where the free front loops parallel the more complex motifs along the border. The motifs are joined as you go, and the triangular section is picked up from the top of the motifs, therefore—no sewing!

*Diagram A*

Beginning of Lower Shawl Body

Last Motif

## NOTES

- For instructions on **Half Double Crochet 2 Together (hdc2tog),** see p. 112.

- When working the body of the shawl, decreases are made over the first two and last two stitches on each row.

*Diagram B*

Lower Shawl Body
Row 2 at Junction
Between Motifs

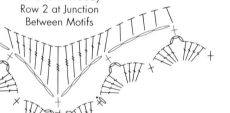

*Diagram C*

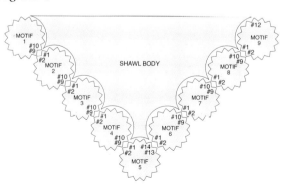

## Stitch Key

⬭ = chain (ch)

• = slip stitch (sl st)

+ = single crochet (sc)

T = half double crochet (hdc)

⊤ = double crochet (dc)

⊤ = treble crochet (tr)

⊤ = double treble crochet (dtr)

## MEDALLION MOTIF (make 9)

See Diagram A at left for assistance.

With smaller hook, ch 5, join with sl st to form ring.

**RND 1:** Ch 3 (counts as dc), 15 dc in ring, join with sl st to top of beg ch-3—16 sts.

**RND 2:** Ch 3 (counts as dc), 2 dc in same st as joining, [ch 1, sk next dc, 3 dc in next dc] 7 times, ch 1, sl st in top of beg ch-3 to join—24 dc.

**RND 3:** Ch 1, sc in same st as joining, [ch 7, sk next dc, sc in next dc, sc in ch-1 sp, sc in next dc] 8 times, omitting last sc, sl st in first sc to join.

**RND 4:** Ch 1, [(sc, hdc, 2 dc, 5 tr, 2 dc, hdc, sc) all in next ch-7 sp, sk next 3 sc] 8 times, sl st in first sc to join.

**RND 5:** Sl st in each of next 5 sts, ch 3 (counts as dc), dc in same st, *(2 dc, ch 3, 2 dc) all in next tr, 2 dc in next tr**, ch 3, sk next 10 sts, 2 dc in next tr; rep from * around, ending at **, ch 1, hdc in top of beg ch-3 to join.

**RND 6:** Ch 7 (counts as tr, ch 3), *(dc, ch 3, dc) all in next ch-3 sp, ch 3, (tr, ch 3, tr) all in next ch-3 sp, ch 3; rep from * around, ending tr in ch-1 sp from end of prev rnd, ch 1, hdc in 4th ch of beg ch-7.

### First Motif

**RND 7:** Ch 1, sc in same sp, *(4 dc, ch 3, 4 dc) all in next ch-3 sp, sc in next ch-3 sp; rep from * around, omitting last sc, sl st in first sc to join. Fasten off.

### Motifs 2–9

*Joining Rnd 7:* Ch 1, sc in same sp, [4 dc in next ch-3 sp, ch 1, with WS together sc in corresponding ch-3 sp of completed motif (see Joining Motifs below), ch 1, 4 dc in same sp on current motif, sc in next ch-3 sp] twice (one side joined), *(4 dc, ch 3, 4 dc) all in next ch-3 sp, sc in next ch-3 sp; rep from * around, omitting last sc, sl st in first sc to join. Fasten off.

### Joining Motifs

Using Diagram C at left as a guide, join motifs on Rnd 7 as follows: Join second motif to any two consecutive points on first completed motif. For motifs 2–5, join point #1 to point #10 on adjacent motif and point #2 to point #9. For motif 6, counting counterclockwise join point #1 to point #14 on motif #5, and point #2 to point #13 (corner made). Join rem motifs as for motifs 2–5.

## LOWER SHAWL BODY

See Diagrams A and B and schematic on p. 74 for assistance.

ROW 1: Beg with last motif joined and using larger hook, join yarn with sl st to ch-3 sp on point #12, ch 1, sc into same sp, [ch 4, sc into next ch-3 sp] 4 times, ch 4, sc into sc sp that joins motifs tog, *[ch 4, sc into next ch-3 sp] 6 times, ch 4, sc into sc sp that joins motifs tog* rep from * to * 2 more times, [ch 4, sc into next ch-3 sp] 2 times, ch 4, sc into sc sp that joins motifs tog, rep from * to * 3 times, [ch 4, sc into next ch-3 sp] 5 times, turn—55 ch-4 sps.

ROW 2: Ch 1, hdc in 1st st, 4 hdc in next ch-4 sp, [hdc in next sc, 4 hdc in next ch-4 sp] 3 times. *hdc in next sc, (3 dc, 2 tr, dtr) all in next ch-4 sp, dtr in next sc, (dtr, 2 tr, 3 dc) all in next ch-4 sp, [hdc in next sc, 4 hdc in ch-4 sp] 5 times*; rep from * to * 2 more times, hdc in next sc, (3 dc, 2 tr, dtr) all in next ch-4 sp, dtr in next sc, (dtr, 2 tr, 3 dc) all in next ch-4 sp, hdc in next sc, 4 hdc in next ch-4 sp, rep from * to * 3 times, hdc in next sc, (3 dc, 2 tr, dtr) all in next ch-4 sp, dtr in next sc, (dtr, 2 tr, 3 dc) all in next ch-4 sp, [hdc in next sc, 4 hdc in ch-4 sp] 4 times, hdc in next sc, turn—308 sts.

ROWS 3–4: Ch 1, hdc-blo in each st across, turn.

ROW 5: Ch 1, hdc2tog-blo, hdc-blo in each of next 149 sts, [hdc2tog-blo] 3 times, hdc-blo in each of next 149 sts, hdc2tog-blo, turn—303 hdc.

ROW 6: Ch 1, hdc2tog-blo, hdc-blo in each of the next 146 sts, [hdc2tog-blo] 3 times, hdc-blo in each of the next 147 sts, hdc2tog-blo, turn—298 sts.

ROW 7: Ch 1, hdc2tog-blo, hdc-blo in each of the next 144 sts, [hdc2tog-blo] 3 times, hdc-blo in each of the next 144 sts, hdc2tog-blo, turn—293 sts.

ROW 8: Ch 1, hdc2tog-blo, hdc-blo in each of the next 142 sts, [hdc2tog-blo] 3 times, hdc-blo in each of the next 141 sts, hdc2tog-blo, turn—288 sts.

ROW 9: Ch 1, hdc2tog-blo, hdc-blo in each of the next 139 sts, [hdc2tog-blo] 3 times, hdc-blo in each of the next 139 sts, hdc2tog-blo, turn—283 sts.

ROW 10: Ch 1, hdc2tog-blo, hdc-blo in each of the next 136 sts, [hdc2tog-blo] 3 times, hdc-blo in each of the next 137 sts, hdc2tog-blo, turn—278 sts.

ROW 11: Ch 1, hdc2tog-blo, hdc-blo in each of the next 134 sts, [hdc2tog-blo] 3 times, hdc-blo in each of the next 134 sts, hdc2tog-blo, turn—273 sts.

ROW 12: Ch 1, hdc2tog-blo, hdc-blo in each of the next 132 sts, [hdc2tog-blo] 3 times, hdc-blo in each of the next 131 sts, hdc2tog-blo, turn—268 sts.

ROW 13: Ch 1, hdc2tog-blo, hdc-blo in each of the next 129 sts, [hdc2tog-blo] 3 times, hdc-blo in each of the next 129 sts, hdc2tog-blo, turn—263 sts.

ROW 14: Ch 1, hdc2tog-blo, hdc-blo in each of the next 126 sts, [hdc2tog-blo] 3 times, hdc-blo in each of the next 127 sts, hdc2tog-blo, turn—258 sts.

ROW 15: Ch 1, hdc2tog-blo, hdc-blo in each of the next 124 sts, [hdc2tog-blo] 3 times, hdc-blo in each of the next 124 sts, hdc2tog-blo, turn—253 sts.

ROW 16: Ch 1, hdc2tog-blo, hdc-blo in each of the next 122 sts, [hdc2tog-blo] 3 times, hdc-blo in each of the next 121 sts, hdc2tog-blo, turn—248 sts.

ROW 17: Ch 1, hdc2tog-blo, hdc-blo in each of the next 119 sts, [hdc2tog-blo] 3 times, hdc-blo in each of the next 119 sts, hdc2tog-blo, turn—243 sts.

ROW 18: Ch 1, hdc2tog-blo, hdc-blo in each of the next 116 sts, [hdc2tog-blo] 3 times, hdc-blo in each of the next 117 sts, hdc2tog-blo, turn—238 sts.

ROW 19: Ch 1, hdc2tog-blo, hdc-blo in each of the next 114 sts, [hdc2tog-blo] 3 times, hdc-blo in each of the next 114 sts, hdc2tog-blo, turn—233 sts.

**ROW 20:** Ch 1, hdc2tog-blo, hdc-blo in each of the next 112 sts, [hdc2tog-blo] 3 times, hdc-blo in each of the next 111 sts, hdc2tog-blo, turn—228 sts.

**ROW 21:** Ch 1, hdc2tog-blo, hdc-blo in each of the next 109 sts, [hdc2tog-blo] 3 times, hdc-blo in each of the next 109 sts, hdc2tog-blo, turn—223 sts.

**ROW 22:** Ch 1, hdc2tog-blo, hdc-blo in each of the next 106 sts, [hdc2tog-blo] 3 times, hdc-blo in each of the next 107 sts, hdc2tog-blo, turn—218 sts.

**ROW 23:** Ch 1, hdc2tog-blo, hdc-blo in each of the next 104 sts, [hdc2tog-blo] 3 times, hdc-blo in each of the next 104 sts, hdc2tog-blo, turn—213 sts.

**ROW 24:** Ch 1, hdc2tog-blo, hdc-blo in each of the next 102 sts, [hdc2tog-blo] 3 times, hdc-blo in each of the next 101 sts, hdc2tog-blo, turn—208 sts.

## SHAPE SHOULDERS

**ROW 1:** Ch 1, [hdc2tog-blo, hdc-blo in each of the next 3 sts] 41 times, hdc2tog-blo, hdc-blo, turn—166 sts.

**ROW 2:** Ch 1, hdc2tog-blo, hdc-blo in each of the next 78 sts, [hdc2tog-blo] 3 times, hdc-blo in each of the next 78 sts, hdc2tog-blo, turn—161 sts.

**ROW 3:** Ch 1, hdc2tog-blo, hdc-blo in each of the next 75 sts, [hdc2tog-blo] 3 times, hdc-blo in each of the next 76 sts, hdc2tog-blo, turn—156 sts.

**ROW 4:** Ch 1, hdc2tog-blo, hdc-blo in each of the next 73 sts, [hdc2tog-blo] 3 times, hdc-blo in each of the next 73 sts, hdc2tog-blo, turn—151 sts.

**ROW 5:** Ch 1, [hdc2tog-blo, hdc-blo in each of the next 3 sts] 30 times, hdc-blo, turn—121 sts.

## UPPER BODY

**ROW 1:** Ch 1, hdc2tog-blo, hdc-blo in each of the next 55 sts, [hdc2tog-blo] 3 times, hdc-blo in each of the next 56 sts, hdc2tog-blo, turn—116 sts.

**ROW 2:** Ch 1, hdc2tog-blo, hdc-blo in each of the next 53 sts, [hdc2tog-blo] 3 times, hdc-blo in each of the next 53 sts, hdc2tog-blo, turn—111 sts.

**ROW 3:** Ch 1, hdc2tog-blo, hdc-blo in each of the next 51 sts, [hdc2tog-blo] 3 times, hdc-blo in each of the next 50 sts, hdc2tog-blo, turn—106 sts.

**ROW 4:** Ch 1, hdc2tog-blo, hdc-blo in each of the next 48 sts, [hdc2tog-blo] 3 times, hdc-blo in each of the next 48 sts, hdc2tog-blo, turn—101 sts.

**ROW 5:** Ch 1, hdc2tog-blo, hdc-blo in each of the next 45 sts, [hdc2tog-blo] 3 times, hdc-blo in each of the next 46 sts, hdc2tog-blo, turn—96 sts.

**ROW 6:** Ch 1, hdc2tog-blo, hdc-blo in each of the next 43 sts, [hdc2tog-blo] 3 times, hdc-blo in each of the next 43 sts, hdc2tog-blo, turn—91 sts.

**ROW 7:** Ch 1, hdc2tog-blo, hdc-blo in each of the next 41 sts, [hdc2tog-blo] 3 times, hdc-blo in each of the next 40 sts, hdc2tog-blo, turn—86 sts.

**ROW 8:** Ch 1, hdc2tog-blo, hdc-blo in each of the next 38 sts, [hdc2tog-blo] 3 times, hdc-blo in each of the next 38 sts, hdc2tog-blo, turn—81 sts.

**ROW 9:** Ch 1, hdc2tog-blo, hdc-blo in each of the next 35 sts, [hdc2tog-blo] 3 times, hdc-blo in each of the next 36 sts, hdc2tog-blo, turn—76 sts.

**ROW 10:** Ch 1, hdc2tog-blo, hdc-blo in each of the next 33 sts, [hdc2tog-blo] 3 times, hdc-blo in each of the next 33 sts, hdc2tog-blo, turn—71 sts.

**ROW 11:** Ch 1, hdc2tog-blo, hdc-blo in each of the next 31 sts, [hdc2tog-blo] 3 times, hdc-blo in each of the next 30 sts, hdc2tog-blo, turn—66 sts.

**ROW 12:** Ch 1, hdc2tog-blo, hdc-blo in each of the next 28 sts, [hdc2tog-blo] 3 times, hdc-blo in each of the next 28 sts, hdc2tog-blo, turn—61 sts.

**ROW 13:** Ch 1, hdc2tog-blo, hdc-blo in each of the next 25 sts, [hdc2tog-blo] 3 times, hdc-blo in each of the next 26 sts, hdc2tog-blo, turn—56 sts.

**ROW 14:** Ch 1, hdc2tog-blo, hdc-blo in each of the next 23 sts, [hdc2tog-blo] 3 times, hdc-blo in each of the next 23 sts, hdc2tog-blo, turn—51 sts.

**ROW 15:** Ch 1, hdc2tog-blo, hdc-blo in each of the next 21 sts, [hdc2tog-blo] 3 times, hdc-blo in each of the next 20 sts, hdc2tog-blo, turn—46 sts.

**ROW 16:** Ch 1, hdc2tog-blo, hdc-blo in each of the next 18 sts, [hdc2tog-blo] 3 times, hdc-blo in each of the next 18 sts, hdc2tog-blo, turn—41 sts.

**ROW 17:** Ch 1, hdc2tog-blo, hdc-blo in each of the next 15 sts, [hdc2tog-blo] 3 times, hdc-blo in each of the next 16 sts, hdc2tog-blo, turn—36 sts.

**ROW 18:** Ch 1, hdc2tog-blo, hdc-blo in each of the next 13 sts, [hdc2tog-blo] 3 times, hdc-blo in each of the next 13 sts, hdc2tog-blo, turn—31 sts.

**ROW 19:** Ch 1, hdc2tog-blo, hdc-blo in each of the next 11 sts, [hdc2tog-blo] 3 times, hdc-blo in each of the next 10 sts, hdc2tog-blo, turn—26 sts.

**ROW 20:** Ch 1, hdc2tog-blo, hdc-blo in each of the next 8 sts, [hdc2tog-blo] 3 times, hdc-blo in each of the next 8 sts, hdc2tog-blo, turn—21 sts.

**ROW 21:** Ch 1, hdc2tog-blo, hdc-blo in each of the next 5 sts, [hdc2tog-blo] 3 times, hdc-blo in each of the next 6 sts, hdc2tog-blo, turn—16 sts.

**ROW 22:** Ch 1, hdc2tog-blo, hdc-blo in each of the next 3 sts, [hdc2tog-blo] 3 times, hdc-blo in each of the next 3 sts, hdc2tog-blo, turn—11 sts.

## FINISHING

Fasten off. Weave in loose ends. Handwash, block to finished measurements, and let dry.

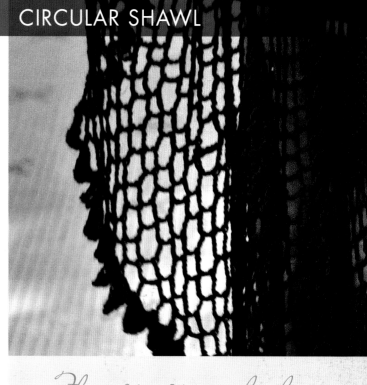

*Stella*

## materials

**YARN:** Worsted weight (#4 Medium), 1,300 yd (1,188.7 m).

*Shown:* Blue Sky Alpacas, Suri Merino (60% baby suri alpaca, 40% merino wool; 164 yd [150 m]/3.5 oz [100 g]): #423 twilight, 8 skeins.

## notions

Tapestry needle
Blocking pins

## hook

H/8 (5mm) or size needed to obtain gauge.

## gauge

14 sts and 16 rows = 4" (10 cm) in sc.

## finished size

64" (162.5 cm) in diameter.

*This intricate circular lace* shawl showcases a beautiful swirling star motif with a picot edging reminiscent of flower petals. It can be worn folded in half for a warm daytime shawl, or it can be worn more dramatically with one third folded over for a shawl collar, allowing the star motif to drape across the back. You can even wear it long, so that the length hangs all the way down your back to create some drama for a night out. Finish it by securing the fronts with a favorite shawl pin or brooch.

*Stella*

**Diagram A**

Rounds 1–30

## NOTES

* The central swirling star motif can be memorized after a couple of rows. Then, the two-row-repeat lace section is worked without increasing in the stitch pattern. All the increases are concentrated within the first row.

* The fabric will appear very ruffled for the first few inches after Row 40, but as the shawl grows larger, the ruffles will relax and lay flat.

### Stitch Key

$\bigcirc$ = chain (ch)

$\bullet$ = slip stitch (sl st)

$+$ = single crochet (sc)

$\top$ = double crochet (dc)

$\ddagger$ = treble crochet (tr)

$\ddagger$ = double treble crochet (dtr)

**Diagram B**

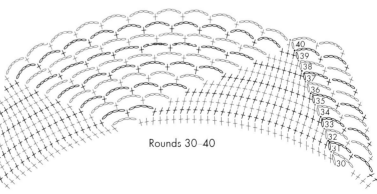

Rounds 30–40

*Diagram C*

Edging

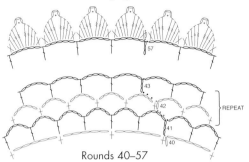

Rounds 40–57

## wrap

See Diagram A at left for assistance.

Ch 8, join with sl st to form ring.

**RND 1:** Ch 1, work 16 sc in ring, sl st in first sc at beg of rnd to join.

**RND 2:** Ch 1, sc in first st, *ch 5, sk next sc, sc in next sc; rep from * around, ending ch 5, sl st in first sc to join—8 ch 5-sps.

**RND 3:** Ch 1, sc in first sc, *work 2 sc in next ch-5 sp, ch 4, sc in next sc; rep from * around, ending ch 4, sl st in first sc to join—8 sections of 3 sc bet ch-4 sps.

**RND 4:** Ch 1, sk first sc, *sc in each of next 2 sc, 2 sc in next ch-4 sp, ch 4, sk first sc of next 3 sc; rep from * around, ending ch 4, sl st in first sc to join—4 sc bet ch-4 sps.

**RNDS 5–30:** Ch 1, sk first sc, *sc in each sc to next ch-4 sp, 2 sc in ch-4 sp, ch 4, sk first sc of next sc section; rep from * around, ending ch 4, sl st in first sc to join—30 sc bet ch-4 sps on last round.

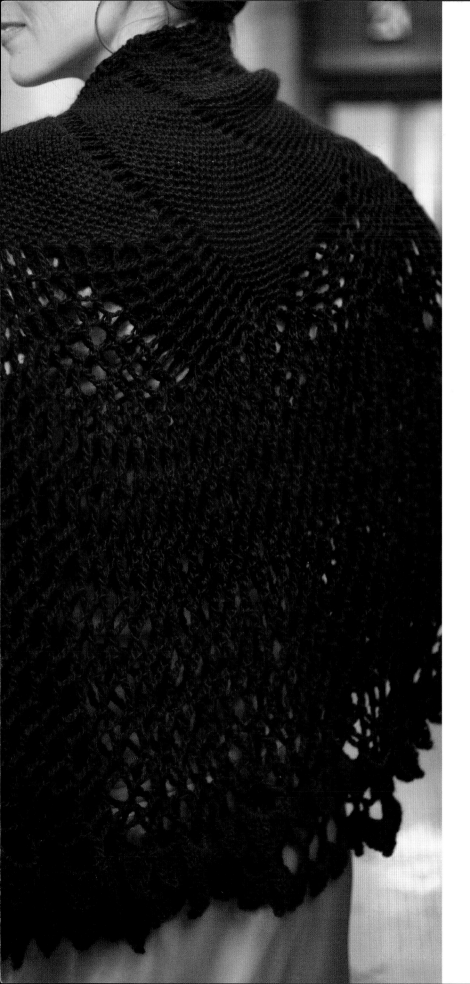

*Note:* See Diagram B on p. 82 for assistance with instructions below.

**RND 31:** Ch 1, sk first sc, *sc in each of next 27 sc, sk next 2 sc, ch 4, sc in next ch-4 sp, ch 4, sk first sc of next section; rep from * around, ending ch 4, sl st in first sc to join—27 sc bet ch-4 sps.

**RND 32:** Ch 1, sk first sc, *sc in each of next 24 sc, sk next 2 sc, [ch 5, sc in next ch-4 sp] twice, ch 5, sk first sc of next section; rep from * around, ending ch 5, sl st in first sc to join—24 sc in each section.

**RNDS 33–39:** Cont in est patt, dec each sc section by 3 sc and adding 1 more ch-5 sp between sections on each rnd—3 sc in each section.

**RND 40:** Ch 1, sk first sc, sc in next sc, *[ch 5, sc in next ch-5 sp] 10 times, ch 5, sc in second sc of next 3-sc section; rep from * around, ending ch 5, sl st in first sc to join.

*Note:* On next rnd, we are doubling the amount of stitches from the prev rnd. This will allow the remainder of the shawl to be worked without inc. See Diagram C on p. 83 for assistance.

**RND 41:** Ch 8 (counts as dc and ch 5), *dc in next ch-5 sp, ch 5, dc in next sc, ch 5; rep from * around, ending ch 5, join with sl st to 3rd ch of beg ch-8.

**RND 42:** Sl st to center of first ch-5 sp, ch 1, sc in same sp, *ch 5, sc in next ch-5 sp; rep from * around, ending ch 5, sl st in first sc to join.

**RND 43:** Sl st to center of first ch-5 sp, ch 8 (counts as dc and ch 5), *dc in next ch-5 sp, ch 5; rep from * around, sl st to 3rd ch of beg ch-8.

**RNDS 44–57:** Rep Rnds 42 and 43 seven more times.

## EDGING

See Diagram C on p. 83 for assistance.

Sl st into first ch-5 sp, ch 1, work (sc, hdc, dc, tr, dtr, ch 3, sl st into 3rd ch from hook (picot made), dtr, tr, dc, hdc, sc) into each ch-5 sp around, sl st into first sc at beg of rnd to join. Fasten off. Weave in loose ends.

## FINISHING

Handwash. Place a pin in the center of the shawl and one pin in the picot center of every petal around the perimeter of the shawl for a perfectly blocked edging. Allow to dry.

# he loves me, he loves me not

## SHAWL WITH FLOWER-PETAL TIERS

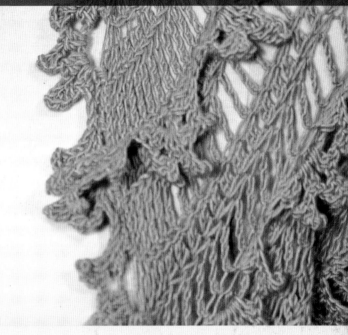

## materials

**YARN:** Dk weight (#3 Light), 1,080 yd (987.6 m).

*Shown:* Classic Elite, Miracle (50% alpaca, 50% Tencel; 108 yd [99 m]/1.75 oz [50 g]): #3362 tea rose, 10 skeins.

## notions

Tapestry needle

## hook

G/6 (4mm) or size needed to obtain gauge.

## gauge

9 sts and 5 rows = 4" (10 cm) in dtr.

## finished size

78" wide x 30" long (198.5 cm x 76 cm).

*I remember taking a flower*
as a child and picking off the petals to determine whether or not a boy was interested in me. He loves me, he loves me not—of course we all know what we wanted to land on at the last petal! This shawl was inspired by those happy childhood memories. I worked through the back loops on the shawl to create an edging with rows and rows of tiny "flower petals." When I look at all of them dangling from the edges, I think about touching each one and reciting those words again.

**Diagram A**

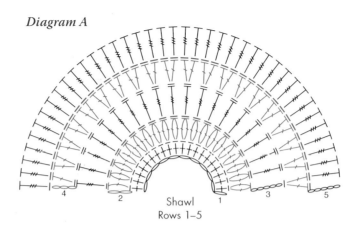

Shawl
Rows 1–5

**Diagram B**

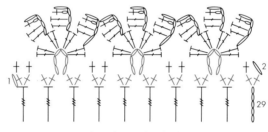

Reduced Sample of Edging

## NOTES

- For instructions on special stitches used in this pattern, see the following pages: **2 Double Crochet Cluster (2-dc cl)**, p. 115; **Extended Single Crochet (Esc)**, p. 115; **3-Petal Flower**, p. 117.

- The cluster rows are worked through the back loops only to give us a great edge (free loop) for adding a lace edging at the end. Notice that because each row alternates between the front loop and the back loop of the stitch, the free loops are all on one side of the shawl.

- When working across the flat edge of the shawl, work evenly across edge, placing 4 sc into the space at the end of each dtr row and 2 sc into the space at the end of each dc row.

*Stitch Key*

⬯ = chain (ch)

• = slip stitch (sl st)

┼ = single crochet (sc)

= extended single crochet (esc)

= double crochet (dc)

= double treble crochet (dtr)

= 2 double crochet cluster (2-dc cl)

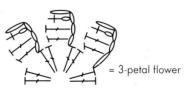 = 3-petal flower

— = worked in back loop only (blo)

▬ = worked in front loop only (flo)

## shawl

See Diagram A above for assistance.

Ch 11.

**ROW 1 (WS):** 2 sc in 2nd ch from hook and in each ch across, turn—20 sc.

**ROW 2:** Working in blo, ch 2, dc in first st (counts as first 2-dc cl), 2-dc cl in next st and each st across, turn.

**ROW 3:** Ch 5 (counts as first dtr), sk first st, dtr-flo in each st across, turn.

**ROW 4:** Ch 3 (counts as first dc), dc-blo in first dtr, 2 dc-blo in next dtr and each dtr across, turn—40 sts.

**ROW 5:** Rep Row 3.

**ROWS 6–9:** Rep Rows 2–5—80 sts.

**ROWS 10–15:** Rep Rows 2–3 three times.

**ROW 16:** Rep Row 4—160 sts.

**ROW 17:** Rep Row 3.

**ROWS 18–29:** Rep Rows 2–3 six times. Do not fasten off.

## EDGING
See Diagram B at left for assistance.

Working across last row worked for shawl:

**ROW 1:** Ch 1, 2 sc in each of first 2 sts, *ch 6, 2 sc in each of next 3 sts; rep from * across to last 2 sts, ch 6, 2 sc in each of last 2 sts, turn—53 ch-6 sps.

**ROW 2:** Ch 1, sk first st, sc in next st, sk next 2 sts, work 3-Petal Flowers across to end, except on last rep, sk 2 sts, sc in each of last 2 sts. Fasten off—53 flowers.

### Working in Free Loops Created on Rows 18, 22, 26:

ROW 1: With RS facing and straight edge of shawl closest to you, join with sl st to free loop of first st, ch 1, sc in same loop, sc in next st, ch 6, *sc in each of next 6 sts, ch 6; rep from * across to last 2 sts, sc in each of last 2 sts, turn—27 ch-6 sps.

ROW 2: Ch 1, sk first 2 sts, work 3-Petal Flower pattern across to end, except on last rep, sk 1 st, sc in last st. Fasten off—27 flowers.

### Working in Free Loops Created on Rows 10 and 14 (with 80 free loops):

ROW 1: With RS facing and straight edge of shawl closest to you, join with sl st to free loop of first st, ch 1, sc in same loop, ch 6, *sc in each of next 6 sts, ch 6; rep from * across to last st, sc in last st, turn—14 ch-6 sps.

ROW 2: Ch 1, skip 1st st, work 3-Petal Flowers across to end, except on last rep, sc in last st. Fasten off—14 flowers.

### Working in Free Loops Created on Row 6 (rows with 40 free loops):

ROW 1: With RS facing and straight edge of shawl closest to you, join with sl st to free loop of first st, ch 1, sc in same loop, sc in next st, ch 6, *sc in each of next 6 sts, ch 6; rep from * across to last 2 sts, sc in each of last 2 sts, turn—27 ch-6 sps.

ROW 2: Ch 1, sk first 2 sts, work 3-Petal Flowers across to end, except on last rep, sk 1 st, sc in last st. Fasten off—27 flowers.

### BORDER

With RS facing and working across straight edge, join yarn with sl st at end of last dtr row worked in main patt, ch 1, 4 sc in same sp, 2 sc in end of next cl row, ch 6, *4 sc in end of next dtr row, 2 sc in end of next cl row, ch 6; rep from * across to foundation ch, work 2 sc in bottom loop of first ch, sc in each of next 4 ch, ch 6, sc in each of next 4 ch, 2 sc in last ch, ch 6, rep from * across rem edge to end, working 4 sc in end of last dtr row—about 58 ch-6 sps.

*Next Row:* Ch 1, sk 1st sc, sc in next st, sk next st, work 3-Petal Flowers across to end, except on last rep, sk 1 st, sc in each of last 2 sts. Fasten off—about 58 flowers.

### FINISHING

Handwash, block to finished measurements, and let dry.

*farrah*

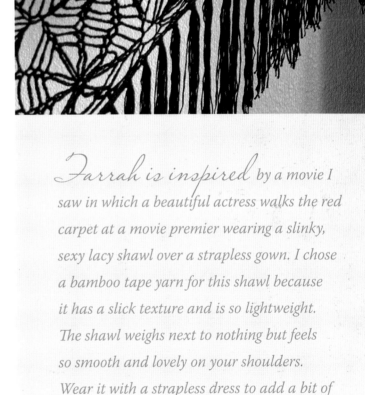

## materials

**YARN:** Fingering weight (#1 Super Fine), 900 yd (823 m).

*Shown:* Naturally, Stella (100% bamboo; 191 yd [175 m]/1.75 oz [50 g]): #11 black, 5 balls.

## notions

Tapestry needle
Split-ring stitch marker

## hook

G/6 (4mm) or size needed to obtain gauge.

## gauge

Blocked square motif = 6" (15 cm) square.

## finished size

60" wide x 30" long (152.5 cm x 76 cm), not including fringe.

*Farrah is inspired* by a movie I saw in which a beautiful actress walks the red carpet at a movie premier wearing a slinky, sexy lacy shawl over a strapless gown. I chose a bamboo tape yarn for this shawl because it has a slick texture and is so lightweight. The shawl weighs next to nothing but feels so smooth and lovely on your shoulders. Wear it with a strapless dress to add a bit of Hollywood glamour to your evening.

**Diagram A**

*Stitch Key*

⬭ = chain (ch)

• = slip stitch (sl st)

✛ = single crochet (sc)

⊤ = double crochet (dc)

╪ = double treble crochet (dtr)

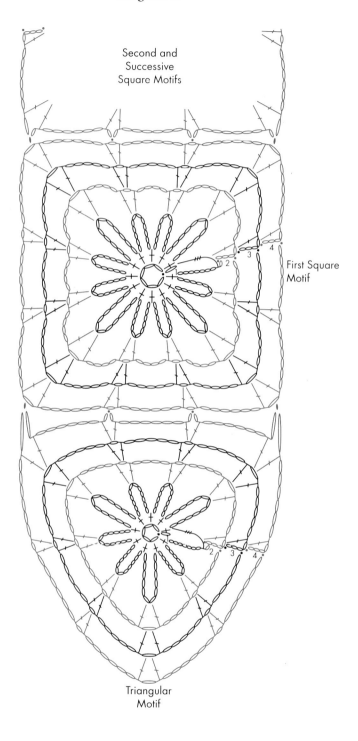

Second and Successive Square Motifs

First Square Motif

Triangular Motif

## NOTE

When choosing a yarn for fringe, cut a sample and look at the ends. You want something that doesn't easily fray. A ribbon or tape yarn, like the one used here, works very well.

## Construction Diagram

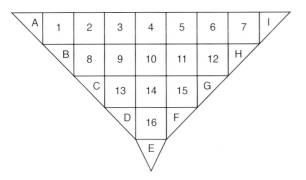

# shawl

Motifs are joined as you go. Begin with First Square Motif (1), then make and join square motifs 2–16 in order according to Construction Diagram above, using instructions for joining one or two sides when necessary. Continue to make and join triangle motifs A-I along side edges of shawl.

## SQUARE MOTIF

### First Square Motif:

See Diagram A at left for assistance.

Ch 6, sl st into first ch to make ring.

**RND 1:** Ch 1, [sc in ring, ch 12] 11 times, sc in ring, ch 7, dtr in ring (counts as ch-12 sp)—12 ch-12 sps.

**RND 2:** Ch 1, sl st into first sp, ch 4 (counts as dc and ch 1), dc in same sp, *ch 4, (dc, ch 1, dc) in next ch-12 sp; rep from * 10 more times, ch 4, sl st into 3rd ch from beg of rnd.

**RND 3:** Sl st into first ch-1 sp, ch 4 (counts as dc and ch 1), dc in same sp, *ch 5, (dc, ch 1, dc) in next ch-1 sp; rep from * 10 more times, ch 5, sl st into 3rd ch from beg of rnd.

**RND 4:** Sl st into first ch-1 sp, ch 4 (counts as dc and ch 1), dc in same sp, *ch 6, (dc, ch 1, dc) in next ch-1 sp; rep from * 10 more times, ch 6, sl st into 3rd ch from beg of rnd. Fasten off.

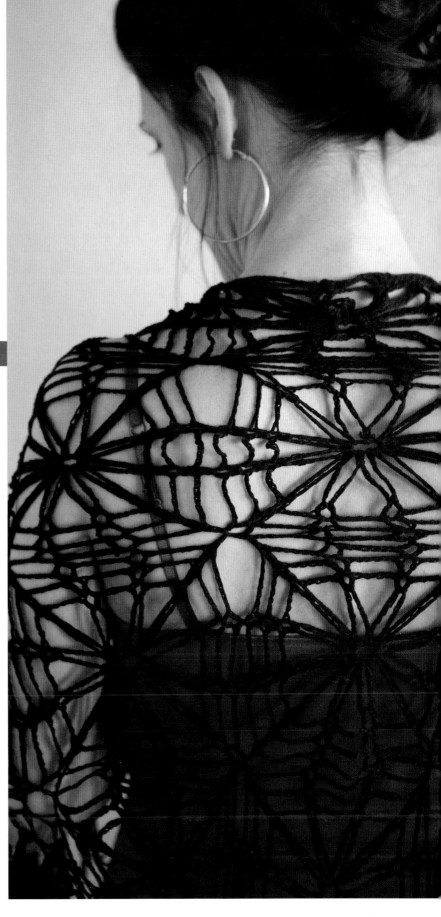

### Joining One Side of Square Motif

**ROWS 1–3:** Rep as for First Square Motif.

**ROW 4:** Sl st into first ch-1 sp, ch 4 (counts as dc and ch 1), dc in same sp, *ch 6, dc in next ch-1 sp, ch 1, sl st into corresponding ch-1 sp of adjacent square, ch 1, dc in same ch-1 sp of current square; rep from * 3 more times, [ch 6, (dc, ch 1, dc) in next ch-1 sp] 7 times, ch 6, sl st into 3rd ch from beg of rnd. Fasten off.

### Joining Two Sides of Square Motif

**ROW 1–3:** Rep as for First Square Motif.

**ROW 4:** Sl st into first ch-1 sp, ch 4 (counts as dc and ch 1), dc in same sp, *ch 6, dc in next ch-1 sp, ch 1, sl st into corresponding ch-1 sp of adjacent square, ch 1, dc in same ch-1 sp of current square; rep from * 6 more times, [ch 6, (dc, ch 1, dc) in next ch-1 sp] 4 times, ch 6, sl st into 3rd ch from beg of rnd. Fasten off.

## TRIANGLE MOTIF

Ch 5, sl st into first ch to make ring.

**RND 1:** Ch 1, [sc in ring, ch 12] 8 times, sc in ring, ch 7, dtr in ring (counts as ch-12 sp)—9 ch-12 sps.

**RND 2:** Ch 1, sl st into first sp, ch 4 (counts as dc and ch 1), dc in same sp,*ch 4, (dc, ch 1, dc) in next ch-12 sp; rep from * 7 more times, ch 4, sl st into 3rd ch from beg of rnd.

**RND 3:** Sl st into first ch-1 sp, ch 4 (counts as dc and ch 1), dc into same sp, *ch 5, (dc, ch 1, dc) in next ch-1 sp; rep from * 7 more times, ch 5, sl st into 3rd ch from beg of rnd.

*Joining Rnd 4:* Sl st into first ch-1 sp, ch 4 (counts as dc and ch 1), dc in same sp, *ch 6, dc in next ch-1 sp, ch 1, sl st into corresponding ch-1 sp of adjacent square, ch 1, dc in same ch-1 sp of current motif; rep from * 3 more times, [ch 6, (dc, ch 1, dc) in next ch-1 sp] 4 times, ch 6, sl st into 3rd ch from beg of rnd. Fasten off.

## FINISHING

### Edging

Once shawl motifs are all assembled, work edging into each ch-sp along the two side edges of the shawl, leaving the top side untouched.

**ROW 1:** With RS facing and beg at top of left edge, join with sl st to outside corner of triangle motif A, (ch 3, sc) into each ch-sp along side to bottom most point of motif E, work ch 3, sc into same sp at point, pm in this ch-3 sp, work (ch 3, sc) into each ch-sp along opposite side to outside corner of motif I, turn—75 ch-3 sps.

**ROW 2:** Sl st into ch-sp, ch 5, sc into same sp, (ch 3, sc) into each ch-3 sp across to marker, work (ch 3, sc) into same sp (move marker to this ch-3 sp), (ch 3, sc) into each ch-3 sp across to end, turn.

**ROW 3:** Rep Row 2. Fasten off and weave in ends.

### Fringe

Cut 600 pieces of yarn, each 18" (45.5 cm) long. Holding 8 strands together in your hand, fold them in half. Pull the folded edge halfway through one of the ch sps. Thread the tail ends through the loop created by the folded edge and bring them all the way through, pulling snugly to fasten the fringe. Repeat for each ch-3 sp across bottom "V" of shawl. Trim edges if necessary.

Handwash, block to measurements, and let dry.

# TRIANGLE-MOTIF SQUARE SHAWL

## materials

**YARN:** Worsted weight (#4 Medium), 190 yd (173.7 m) ea A–K, M; 380 yd (347.5 m) L—2,470 yd (2,258.6 m) total.

*Shown:* Brown Sheep Company, Lamb's Pride Worsted (85% wool, 15% mohair; 190 yd [174 m]/4 oz [112 g]): M03 gray heather (A); M07 sable (B); M175 bronze patina (C); M181 prairie fire (D); M160 dynamite blue (E); M04 charcoal heather (F); M22 autumn harvest (G); M34 victorian pink (H); M124 persian peacock (I); M08 wild oak (J); M01 sandy heather (K); M05 onyx (L); M47 tahiti teal (M), 1 ball of each color, except 2 balls of onyx (L).

## notions

Tapestry needle

## hook

H/8 (5mm) or size needed to obtain gauge.

## gauge

1 triangle motif = 6" wide at base x 6" tall (15 cm x 15 cm).

## finished size

30" (76 cm) square.

*Inspired by the palette of a* Native American painting, the colors used in this shawl were chosen to symbolize different earthly elements: fire, water, earth, and air. The sun and moon are also represented. To make the shawl, I invited several women together for an evening of crocheting motifs. We ate, drank, and crocheted for hours. It was really fun, and we finished all the motifs! This would be an amazing gift for a group of crocheters to collectively give to someone special—a mother, a grandmother, or a close friend.

## Diagram A

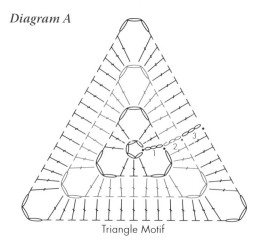

Triangle Motif

### Stitch Key

◯ = chain (ch)

• = slip stitch (sl st)

╪ = double crochet (dc)

*mother nature*

### NOTES

※ When laying out motifs, it may be helpful to pin a few motifs together at the beginning.

※ To create the black "piping" look of the seams, join motifs together with sc through both thicknesses, working through the inside loops of each motif.

※ A shawl pin would make a great closure for this garment. You could also sew a button at the top and make a button loop by chaining a loop (about as long as the button) on the opposite side.

### Construction Diagram

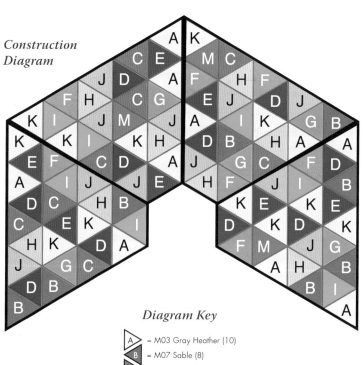

### Diagram Key

A = M03 Gray Heather (10)
B = M07 Sable (8)
C = M175 Bronze Patina (8)
D = M181 Prairie Fire (10)
E = M160 Dynamite Blue (7)
F = M04 Charcoal Heather (7)
G = M22 Autumn Harvest (5)
H = M34 Victorian Pink (8)
I = M124 Persian Peacock (7)
J = M08 Wild Oak (11)
K = M01 Sandy Heather (12)
M = M47 Tahiti Teal (3)

*Diagram B*

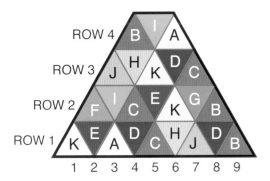

TRIANGLE MOTIF *(make 96)*
See Diagram A at left for assistance.

Ch 5, sl st to form ring.

**RND 1:** Ch 3 (counts as dc), working into ring, (2 dc, ch 3, [3 dc, ch 3] twice), sl st to top of beg ch-3—9 dc, 3 ch-3 sps.

**RND 2:** Ch 3 (counts as dc), dc in each of next 2 sts, *(3 dc, ch 3, 3 dc) into next ch-3 sp, dc in each of next 3 sts; rep from * once more, (3 dc, ch 3, 3 dc) into next ch-3 sp, join with sl st to top of ch-3 at beg of rnd—27 dc, 3 ch-3 sps.

**RND 3:** Ch 3 (counts as dc), dc in each of next 5 sts, *(3 dc, ch 3, 3 dc) into next ch-3 sp, dc in each of next 9 sts; rep from * once more, (3 dc, ch 3, 3 dc) into next ch-3 sp, dc in each of next 3 sts, join with sl st to top of ch-3 at beg of rnd—45 dc, 3 ch-3 sps.

Fasten off.

## ASSEMBLY

Look carefully at the Construction Diagram on p. 100: each side of the square cape is a triangle, and each of those triangles is made up of 24 of the Triangle Motifs. Now, notice that the large triangle is broken into 4 sections (delineated by heavier black lines).

### *First Constructed Triangle:*

See Diagram B on p. 101 for assistance.

Beg with Row 1 (bottom row), join motifs 1–9 together (paying attention to the position of each triangle) in the following manner: Holding motifs 1 and 2 together, join L with sl st through the inside loops of first st, ch 1, working through both thicknesses sc in each st across, joining one edge of motif 1 to motif 2, ch 1, rotate to view the next edge of motif 2, holding motifs 2 and 3 together sc in each st across to join the 3rd motif. Continue in this manner until motifs 1–9 are joined (see Construction Diagram for assistance with color placement). Fasten off.

Creating a separate strip for each row of the triangle, rep same technique for joining the 7 motifs in Row 2, the 5 motifs in Row 3, and finally the 3 motifs in Row 4 (top row).

Join strips together to form triangle, as shown in Diagram B on p. 101.

### *Subsequent Constructed Triangles:*

Create three more triangles as for first triangle using Construction Diagram on p. 100 for color placement. You should now have four large triangles constructed of the smaller Triangle Motifs to join. Working through both thicknesses with RS facing, join all four triangles leaving the outside edge of first and last triangle unjoined.

## FINISHING

**RND 1:** With RS facing, join L with sl st to center back of neck, ch 1, sc in each st across to neck corner, 3 sc in corner st, sc in each st along left front edge, 3 sc in corner st, sc in each st across bottom edge, 3 sc in corner st, sc in each st across right front edge, 3 sc in corner st, sc in each st across neck edge to end of rnd, sl st into first st of rnd to join.

**RND 2:** Ch 1, sc in same st, sc in each st around, sl st to first sc to join. Fasten off.

Handwash, block to finished measurements, and let dry.

# hypnotize

## materials

**YARN:** Worsted weight (#4 Medium), 780 yd (713.2 m) A; 450 yd (411.5 m) B—1,230 yd (1,124.7 m) total.

*Shown:* Tilli Tomas, Pure & Simple (100% silk; 260 yd [238 m]/3.5 oz [100 g]): atmosphere (A), 3 skeins.
Tilli Tomas, Disco Lights (100% silk prestrung with petite sequins, 225 yd [206 m]/3.5 oz [100 g]): atmosphere (B), 2 skeins.

## notions

Yarn needle
Stitch markers

## hook

G/6 (4.0mm) or size needed to obtain gauge.

## gauge

10 stitches and 4 rows of dtr = 4" (10 cm) after blocking.

## finished size

60" wide x 28" long (152.5 cm x 71 cm).
Circular center is 20" (51 cm) in diameter.

*I love spirals* and find ways to incorporate them into my crochet whenever I can. For this shawl, working a piping round in sequined silk really accentuates the geometry of the spiral. The sequins are small and subtle, but they shimmer and shine when you move. Imagine a handsome admirer noticing you from across the room and becoming entranced (or even hypnotized) by the sparkling spiral wrapped around your shoulders. It could happen!

*hypnotize*

*Diagram A*

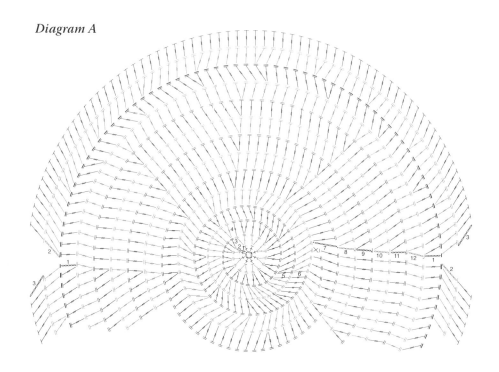

## NOTES

- For instructions on **Reverse Single Crochet (rev sc)**, see p. 114.

- The shawl begins in the center and is worked out to a circular form with a diameter the same size as the desired finished width of the shawl. The remainder of the shawl is worked in rows, on half of the circle, until the finished piece is oval shaped.

- All stitches are worked through back loops only unless otherwise indicated.

- When looking at the right side of the fabric, the goal is to have free loops to work into on every row/round. With the contrast yarn, work a row/round of reverse single crochet in every free loop on the entire shawl in the contrast yarn.

*Stitch Key*

⬭ = chain (ch)

• = slip stitch (sl st)

✝ = single crochet (sc)

╤ = half double crochet (hdc)

╪ = double crochet (dc)

⟊ = treble crochet (tr)

⟊ = double treble crochet (dtr)

— = worked in back loop only (blo)

▬ = worked in front loop only (flo)

## CIRCULAR MOTIF

See Diagram A at left for assistance.

Ch 4, sl st into 1st ch to form ring.

**RND 1 (RS):** Ch 1, work 8 sc into ring, do not join, pm in first st to mark beg of rnd, move marker up with each new rnd—8 sts.

**RND 2:** [2 hdc-blo of next st] 5 times, [2 dc-blo of next st] 3 times—16 sts.

**RND 3:** [2 dc-blo of next st] 6 times, [2 tr-blo of next st] 7 times, tr-blo of next st, 2 tr-blo of next st, tr-blo of next st—30 sts.

**RND 4:** [2 tr-blo of next st, tr-blo in next st] 5 times, [2 tr-blo of next st] 3 times, tr-blo of next st, [2tr-blo of next st] 2 times—40 sts around.

*Note:* You will not have worked in each st from Rnd 3, move marker to next st to move and mark beg of next rnd.

**RND 5:** [2tr-blo in next st, tr-blo in each of next 4 sts] 8 times—48 sts.

**RND 6:** [2dtr-blo in next st, dtr-blo in each of next 5 sts] 8 times—56 sts.

Work tr-blo in next st, dc-blo in next st, hdc-blo in next st, sc-blo in next st, sl st-blo in next st.

**RND 7:** Ch 5 (counts as 1st dtr here and throughout patt), dtr-blo in same st, dtr-blo in each of next 6 sts, [2 dtr-blo in next st, dtr-blo in each of next 6 sts] 7 times, sl st-blo in top of ch-5 to join—64 dtr.

**RND 8:** Ch 5, dtr-blo in same st, dtr-blo in each of next 7 sts, [2 dtr-blo in next st, dtr-blo in each of next 7 sts] 7 times, sl st-blo in top of ch-5 to join—72 sts.

**RND 9:** Ch 5, dtr-blo in same st, dtr-blo in each of next 8 sts, [2dtr-blo in next st, dtr-blo in each of next 8 sts] 7 times, sl st-blo in top of ch-5 to join—80 sts.

**RND 10:** Ch 5, dtr-blo in same st, dtr-blo in each of next 9 sts, [2 dtr-blo in next st, dtr-blo in each of next 9 sts] 7 times, sl st-blo in top of ch-5 to join—88 sts.

**RND 11:** Ch 5, dtr-blo in same st, dtr-blo in each of next 10 sts, [2 dtr-blo in next st, dtr-blo in each of next 10 sts] 7 times, sl st-blo in top of ch-5 to join—96 sts.

**RND 12:** Ch 5, dtr-blo in same st, dtr-blo in each of next 11 sts, [2 dtr-blo in next st, dtr-blo in each of next 11 sts] 7 times, sl st-blo in top of ch-5 to join—104 sts.

# Glossary

## ABBREVIATIONS

| | | | | |
|---|---|---|---|---|
| beg | beginning | | patt | pattern(s) |
| bet | between | | pm | place marker |
| blo | back loop(s) only | | prev | previous |
| bp | back post | | rem | remain(s); remaining |
| bp-cl | back post cluster | | rnd | round |
| bpdc | back post double crochet | | rep | repeat; repeating |
| ch | chain | | RS | right side(s) |
| ch- | chain or space previously made | | rev sc | reverse single crochet |
| cl | cluster | | sc | single crochet |
| cm | centimeter(s) | | sh | shell |
| dc | double crochet | | sk | skip |
| dc cl | double crochet cluster | | sl st | slip(ped) stitch |
| dec | decrease; decreases; decreasing | | sp | space(s) |
| dtr | double treble crochet | | st(s) | stitch(es) |
| esc | extended single crochet | | tch | turning chain |
| est | established | | tog | together |
| fdc | foundation double crochet | | tr | treble crochet |
| flo | front loop(s) only | | v-st | v stitch |
| fp | front post | | WS | wrong side(s) |
| fp-cl | front post cluster | | yd | yard(s) |
| fpdc | front post double crochet | | yo | yarn over |
| fsc | foundation single crochet | | * | repeat starting point |
| g | gram(s) | | ** | repeat all instructions between asterisks |
| hdc | half double crochet | | () | alternate instructions and/or measurements |
| hdc2tog | half double crochet 2 together | | [] | work bracketed instructions specified number of times |
| inc | increase; increases; increasing | | | |
| m | meter(s) | | | |

## GAUGE

The quickest way to check gauge is to make a square of fabric about 4" (10 cm) wide by 4" (10 cm) tall (or motif indicated in pattern for gauge) with the suggested hook size and in the indicated stitch. If your measurements match the measurements of the pattern's gauge, congratulations! If you have too many stitches, try going up a hook size, if you have too few stitches, try going down a hook size. Crochet another swatch with the new hook until your gauge matches what is indicated in the pattern.

If the gauge has been measured after blocking, be sure to wet your swatch and block it before taking measurements to check gauge. Wet blocking drastically effects the gauge measurement, especially in lace stitch work.

## BLOCKING

Blocking is the most important element of properly finished garments. It allows the fabric to relax and ensures proper shape, measurements, and drape of the fabric. After time and wear, you will still want to block your garment after washings to bring it back to the original shape. Remember to treat wool fibers carefully when wetting or washing to block. Avoid felting by staying away from hot water and agitation (from a washing machine or water removal by hand). Also remember to keep synthetic fibers (i.e., acrylic) away from high heat.

### Spray Blocking
Pin the fabric to the specified dimensions (always use rust-proof pins). You can use a blocking board, carpeted flooring, or a bed (the mattress works well for pushing pins into). If you are going to use the floor or a bed, cover them with towels first. Fill a spray bottle with lukewarm water (sometimes I add a drop of mild, wool-sensitive wash to the bottle) and spray the fabric generously. If it is a natural fiber, when it dries, it will keep the shape you created with the pins. If it is a synthetic fabric, it may relax some and won't keep its shape quite as well as a natural fiber.

### Wet Blocking
Gently submerge the fabric in lukewarm water with a bit of mild, wool-sensitive wash. Don't agitate. Let it soak for 20 minutes or longer, to allow the liquid to absorb into the fibers well. Drain the water and gently expel the water from the fabric (pressing between two layers of towels) but do not wring or twist. Lay the fabric out over a fresh, dry towel and roll it up to expel even more water. Pin the piece out to the specified dimensions (see Spray Blocking above). Allow to dry.

### Steam Blocking
Steam relaxes fibers gently and more subtly than the other two methods. It is very effective on synthetics and silks—the steaming creates lovely drape, even in the roughest acrylics! Follow the directions for pinning under Spray Blocking above. Then use a steamer or an iron on the steam setting to steam the entire piece. Be sure to keep the steamer or iron a few inches away from the surface of the garment to avoid damaging the fibers. Allow to dry.

# Crochet Stitches

## CROCHET CHAIN (CH)
Make a slipknot on hook. Yarn over hook and draw it through loop of slipknot. Repeat, drawing yarn through the last loop formed.

*figure 1*

*figure 2*

## SINGLE CROCHET (SC)
Insert hook into a stitch, yarn over hook and draw a loop through stitch (**Figure 1**), yarn over hook and draw it through both loops on hook (**Figure 2**).

*figure 1*

*figure 2*

## HALF DOUBLE CROCHET (HDC)
*Yarn over hook, insert hook into a stitch, yarn over hook and draw a loop through stitch (3 loops on hook), yarn over hook (**Figure 1**) and draw it through all the loops on the hook (**Figure 2**). Repeat from * for desired number of stitches.

## DOUBLE CROCHET (DC)

*Yarn over hook, insert hook into a stitch (**Figure 1**), yarn over hook and draw a loop through stitch (3 loops on hook), yarn over hook and draw it through 2 loops (**Figure 2**), yarn over hook and draw it through the remaining 2 loops (**Figure 3**). Repeat from * for desired number of stitches.

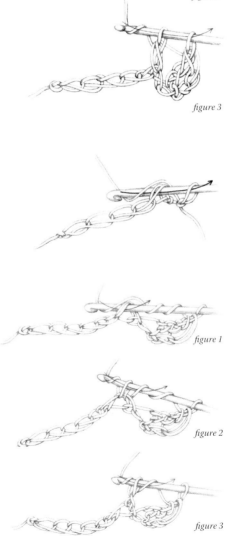

*figure 1*

*figure 2*

*figure 3*

## SLIP STITCH (SL ST)

*Insert hook into stitch, yarn over hook and draw loop through stitch and loop on hook. Repeat from *.

## TREBLE CROCHET (TR)

*Wrap yarn around hook two times, insert hook into a stitch, yarn over hook and draw a loop through stitch (4 loops on hook; **Figure 1**), yarn over hook and draw it through 2 loops (**Figure 2**), yarn over hook and draw it through the next 2 loops (**Figure 3**), yarn over hook and draw it through the remaining 2 loops. Repeat from * for desired number of stitches.

### Double Treble Crochet (dtr)

Wrap yarn around hook three times, insert hook into a stitch. Yarn over hook and draw a loop through stitch. *Yarn over hook and draw it through 2 loops. Repeat from * 3 times.

*figure 1*

*figure 2*

*figure 3*

# Special Stitches

### BACK POST CLUSTER (BP-CL)

*Yarn over hook, insert hook from back to front around post of next st, yarn over hook and pull up a loop, yarn over hook and draw through 2 loops on hook; rep from * once more, yarn over hook and draw through all 3 loops on hook.

### BACK POST DOUBLE CROCHET (BPDC)

Yarn over hook, insert hook from back to front around post of st, yarn over hook and pull up a loop (3 loops on hook), [yarn over hook and draw through 2 loops on hook] twice.

### BROOMSTICK LACE PATTERN
### (BROOMSTICK LACE PATT)

**ROW 1:** Pull loop on hook long enough to place onto knitting needle and remove hook, *insert hook into next st, yarn over hook, pull up loop and place onto knitting needle, remove hook; rep from * across.

**ROW 2:** Insert hook into first 6 loops on knitting needle and slide off of knitting needle, yarn over hook and pull loop through all 6 loops on hook, ch 1 to secure loops, work 6 sc into center sp of 6-loop group, *insert hook into next 6 loops and slide off of knitting needle, yarn over hook and draw through all 6 loops, ch 1, 6 sc into center sp; rep from * across.

**ROW 3:** Rep Row 1.

**ROW 4:** Insert hook into first 3 loops on knitting needle and slide off of knitting needle, yarn over hook and pull loop through all 3 loops, ch 1, 3 sc into center sp, *insert hook into next 6 loops and slide off of knitting needle, yarn over hook and pull loop through all 6 loops, ch 1, 6 sc into center sp; rep from * across to last 3 sts, insert hook into last 3 loops on knitting needle and slide off of knitting needle, yarn over hook and pull loop through all 3 loops, ch 1, 3 sc into center sp.

Rep Rows 1–4 for patt.

### 4-DC BOBBLE

Yarn over hook, insert hook in next sp, yarn over hook, draw up loop, yarn over hook and pull through 2 loops on hook, [yarn over hook, insert hook in same sp, yarn over hook, draw up loop, yarn over hook and draw through 2 loops on hook] 3 times, yarn over hook and draw through all loops on hook.

### 5-DC BOBBLE

Yarn over hook, insert hook in next sp, yarn over hook, draw up loop, yarn over hook and pull through 2 loops on hook, [yarn over hook, insert hook in same sp, yarn over hook, draw up loop, yarn over hook and draw through 2 loops on hook] 4 times, yarn over hook and draw through all loops on hook.

### 2-DC CLUSTER (2-DC CL)

Yarn over hook, insert hook in st, yarn over hook, draw up loop, yarn over hook and draw through two loops on hook, yarn over hook, insert hook in same st, yarn over hook, draw up loop, yarn over hook and draw through two loops on hook, yarn over hook and draw through all 3 loops on hook.

### EXTENDED SINGLE CROCHET (ESC)

Insert hook in next st, yarn over hook, draw up a loop (2 loops on hook), yarn over hook and draw through first loop on hook, yarn over hook and draw through both loops on hook—1 esc made.

### FOUNDATION SINGLE CROCHET (FSC)

Ch 2, insert hook in 2nd ch from hook, yarn over hook and draw up a loop (2 loops on hook), yarn over hook, draw through first loop on hook (chain made), yarn over hook and draw through 2 loops on hook.

*Insert hook under 2 loops of ch made at base of previous st, yarn over hook and draw up a loop (2 loops on hook), yarn over hook and draw through first loop on hook, yarn over hook and draw through 2 loops on hook. Rep from * for length of foundation.

### FOUNDATION DOUBLE CROCHET (FDC)
Ch 3, yarn over hook, insert hook in 3rd ch from hook, yarn over hook and draw up a loop (3 loops on hook), yarn over hook, draw through first loop on hook (chain made), [yarn over hook and draw through 2 loops] twice.

*Yarn over hook, insert hook under both loops of ch just made. Yarn over hook and draw up a loop (3 loops on hook), yarn over hook and draw through 1 loop, [yarn over hook and draw through 2 loops] twice. Rep from * for length of foundation.

### FRONT POST CLUSTER (FP-CL)
*Yarn over hook, insert hook from front to back around post of next st, yarn over hook and pull up a loop, yarn over hook and draw through 2 loops on hook; rep from * once more, yarn over hook and draw through all 3 loops on hook.

### FRONT POST DOUBLE CROCHET (FPDC)
Yarn over hook, insert hook from front to back around post of st indicated, yarn over hook and pull up a loop (3 loops on hook), [yarn over hook and draw through 2 loops on hook] twice.

### FUR STITCH (FUR ST)
Insert hook in st, wrap yarn around index finger of left hand so you have one thread of the loop in front of the left finger and one thread of the loop behind the finger, swing hook over front thread from left to right clockwise, using hook grab both threads of the loop (two strands hooked), and pull through st, drop loop to backside, yarn over hook and draw through remaining loops on hook (1 loop at back side of work and 1 sc made).

### HALF DOUBLE CROCHET 2 TOGETHER (HDC2TOG)
Work a hdc into the next st without completing the very last step (keep all 3 loops on hook), then hdc in the next st without completing the last step. You should have 5 loops on the hook, then yarn over hook and draw through all loops on hook.

dc-tlb: Through back loops only (tbl), wrap the yarn over the hook and insert the hook into the work (or fourth chain from hook). Wrap the yarn over the hook, draw through the work only and wrap the yarn again. Draw through the first two loops only and wrap the yarn again. Draw through the last two loops on the hook.

### 3-PETAL FLOWER

*2 dc into next ch-6 sp, [ch 4, esc in 2nd ch from hook, dc in each of next 2 ch, 2 dc into same ch-6 sp] 3 times (one 3-petal flower made), skip next 2 sts, sc in each of next 2 sts, skip next 2 sts; rep from * for patt.

### PUFF STITCH (PUFF ST)

Work 3 hdc into the same stitch, keeping the top loop of each one on the hook (4 loops on hook). Yarn over hook and draw through all loops on hook (1 puff st made).

### REVERSE SINGLE CROCHET (REV SC)

Working from left to right, insert hook into next stitch, yarn over hook, draw loop of yarn to front of work, yarn over hook and draw through both loops on hook.

### SHELL (SH)

[Tr, ch 1] 5 times in same st.

### V STITCH (V-ST)

(Tr, ch 3, tr) in sp indicated.

# Resources

**Blue Sky Alpacas Inc.**
PO Box 88
Cedar, MN 55011
blueskyalpacas.com
*Alpaca Silk*
*Suri Merino*

**Brown Sheep Yarn Company**
100662 County Road 16
Mitchell, NE 69357
brownsheep.com
*Lamb's Pride Worsted*

**Caron International**
PO Box 222
Washington, NC 27889
caron.com
*Simply Soft, Heather*

**Classic Elite Yarn Company**
122 Western Avenue
Lowell, MA 01851-1434
classiceliteyarns.com
*Miracle*

**Fiber Trends/ Naturally New Zealand Yarn Company**
(888) 733-5991
fibertrends.com
*Natural, Naturelle 8 Ply*
*Natural, Stella*

**Malabrigo Yarn Company**
(786) 866-6187
malabrigoyarn.com
*Merino Lace*

**Muench Yarn Company**
1323 Scott Street
Petaluma, CA 94954-1153
muenchyarns.com
*GGH Soft Kid*

**Patons Yarn**
320 Livingstone Avenue South
Listowel, ON Canada
N4W 3H3
patonsyarns.com
*SWS*
*Grace*

**Plymouth Yarn Company Inc.**
500 Lafayette Street
Bristol, PA 19007
plymouthyarn.com
*Encore Chunky*

**Rowan (dist. by Westminster Fibers)**
165 Ledge Street
Nashua, NH 03060
knitrowan.com
*Kidsilk Haze*
*Bamboo Tape*

**Tahki Stacy Charles Inc.**
70-30 80th Street, Building 36
Ridgewood, NY 11385
tahkistacycharles.com
*Filatura di Crosa, Ariel*
*Loop-d-Loop, Fern*

**Tilli Tomas**
72 Woodland Road
Jamaica Plain, MA 02130
tillitomas.com
*Pure & Simple*
*Disco Lights*

**Trendsetter Yarns**
16745 Satiscoy Street
Suite #101
Van Nuys, CA 91406
trendsetteryarns.com
*Tonalita*

# Index

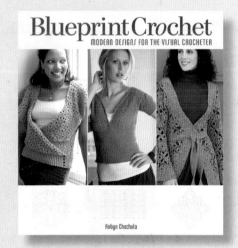

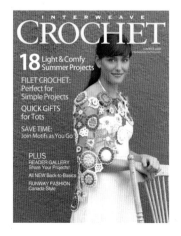